# Pastoral **Peculiars**
## curiosities in the countryside

**Peter Ashley**

ENGLISH HERITAGE

Published by English Heritage, Isambard House, Kemble Drive, Swindon SN2 2GZ
www.english-heritage.org.uk
English Heritage is the Government's statutory adviser on all aspects of the historic
environment.

© Peter Ashley
Preface © Richard Mabey

All images © Peter Ashley, except the following: p 9 Elizabeth Orcutt; p 11; p 21 © Crown
copyright Ordnance Survey; p 22 *Tess of the d'Urbervilles*, Thomas Hardy, Wessex Edition,
Macmillan 1925; p 31 *The Green Roads of England* and *Murray's Berkshire Architectural Guide*;
p 67 Black Treacle can courtesy of Tate & Lyle; p 70 *The Wonder Book of Electricity*; p 100
*British Trains*; and p 107 R101 archive image courtesy of Mary Evans Picture Library.

*The Pylons*, from *New Collected Poems* by Stephen Spender © 2004. Reprinted by kind
permission of the Estate of Sir Stephen Spender.

Every effort has been made to trace copyright holders and we apologise in advance for
any unintentional omissions, which we would be pleased to correct in any subsequent
edition of this book.

First published 2005

ISBN-10 1 85074 960 4
ISBN-13 978 1 85074 960 8
Product code 51059

*British Library Cataloguing in Publication Data*
A CIP catalogue record for this book is available from the British Library.

Edited and brought to press by René Rodgers, English Heritage Publishing
Page layout by Peter Ashley and George Hammond
Cover by Peter Ashley

Printed in the United Kingdom by Hawthornes

This book is dedicated
to all those who look beyond the
obvious, whose curiosity is continually
aroused by the odd and the unfamiliar
in the English landscape.

# contents

**THORPE ACHURCH, NORTHAMPTONSHIRE**

Lilford church was demolished in 1778 and a selection of the stones was re-erected down near the River Nene below Thorpe Achurch: a very deliberate and picturesque eyecatcher.

## preface

The English countryside lies under oppressive mantles today. Not just the grinding yoke of industrial agriculture, but the huge weight of our expectations. Off-the-peg barley-prairie or ancient upland crag, it's all expected to deliver solemnity and symbol – to be immemorial, a bit of This Sceptered Isle, a Land of Lost Content. And these days, in the eyes of its self-elected spokespersons, to be the last refuge of national identity and consensus. Thank goodness for Peter Ashley, court jester to the landscape. Prowling the countryside like a subversive dowser, he uncovers veins of eccentricity and humour and sheer local tanginess that are much more convincing as measures of the spirits of place. Sheltering from a storm under a giant hogweed, he is confronted by a naked figure of Mercury. He overhears stories about a hut near John Betjeman's grave being a makeshift mortuary for drowned sailors. He glimpses scarecrows dressed like Rupert Bear, chapels and chimneys marooned in vast fields, a private observatory that was converted to a windmill and then a grandstand for point-to-points. And a litany of place-names that captures the bizarre, heartening chaos of it all. Caution Corner! What happened there? What, spotting this arresting road sign, is one supposed to *do*?

The countryside has always been a place of devilment. Squatters, sculptors, extravagant squires – those who've occupied and worked there have always wanted to leave some kind of signature, a personal landmark. And often to be elusive, enigmatic, out for mischief. If Peter Ashley is part diviner, part photographic hunter-gatherer, his landscape-makers are like canny prey animals, leaving their tantalising spoors in the most unlikely places. Together they weave a picture of an England where art, craft and nature begin to meld into each other. An abandoned combine harvester, isolated in a photograph, becomes an *objet trouvé*, rusting into new significance. A wild cluster of follies has the feel of the bric-a-brac gathered by bower-birds to ornament their nests.

Peter has, in the best sense, a child's vision of the landscape. What he sees are the mysteries and ghosts and jokes we all once imagined there, made flesh. The recycled railway carriages of the South Coast plotlands echo the romance of childhood dens, the magic of making the world anew. The Lightning fighter rotting away outside a derelict scrapyard by the A1 (it was an advertising gimmick once) makes me remember searching for scraps of crashed planes after the last war and all the guilty exultancy that went with it. Paul Nash's wartime paintings catch the same ambivalent feelings.

Vernacular landscaping is a great debunker of the pomposity of power and ideology. The Cerne Abbas giant may be prehistoric, but modern excavation has shown that its immense phallus only dates from the 18th century, when a gang of doubtless tipsy 'scourers', out to scandalise the local clergy, joined up a more modest organ with the giant's belly-button. In the Chilterns I remember walking behind a pair of ramblers earnestly debating the prehistoric origins (as 'glacial erratics') of a row of pre-cast concrete tank-traps, which my own dad's army had trundled into position just 50 years before. And, in a way, they were right: they were a kind of new erratic. We make the landscape anew in our imaginations. It's just that some of us re-imagine it for real, out in the fields.

What touches me most about Peter's wry and insightful portraits of these 'pastoral peculiars' is how *natural* they seem. However grand their beginnings, however incongruous their settings, what survives in them is their inventiveness and opportunism and idiosyncrasy – the recipe for survival, after all, throughout the rest of creation.

Richard Mabey

In my childhood I kept stowed away amongst my treasures a little yellow book. It was a piece of road safety propaganda – much needed at the time – and consisted of nine luridly coloured pictures of possible major traffic accidents, all tantalisingly close to happening. One depicted an open-topped sports car hurtling along a narrow country lane and in the passenger seat a woman is seen distracting the male driver by shouting out 'Look! Stonehenge!' so that he fails to see a herd of Friesian cows lumbering across the road in front. It made such an impression on me that later, when my father purchased our first car, I sat rigidly in the back willing him to keep his eyes on the road instead of pointing with a driving gloved finger at various sights in the fields on either side of our progression. Eventually, when I realised that there was an even chance that we wouldn't plough the Ford Popular into herds of stray farmyard animals, I started to look nervously out of my own window and the first entries in a catalogue of 'pastoral peculiars' were mentally jotted down.

At first it was probably the stilted leaning figures dressed in worn tweeds, arms outstretched over ploughed furrows ostensibly frightening crows, one of whose sinister number was invariably perched on a battered trilby or panama. And then the isolated towers that grabbed not only attention but the imagination as they played peekaboo behind woods and the curves of hillsides, always engendering the thought that maybe someone – perhaps in a black frock coat holding a brass telescope – was up there on a turret watching us appearing and disappearing far down below. And the equally puzzling landmarks cut into downland chalk: a stylised trademark of a horse, a priapic giant, a row of regimental badges lined up as if pinned on an olive drab uniform. A human attempt to subdue the landscape, to leave a mark.

These were the most noticeable, the most obvious. Later, as I walked the fields and climbed the hills, other oddities came into view or slowly revealed themselves. Isolated churches left marooned in fields far from their villages and ruined churches robbed of their parishes altogether. Strange reminders of landowners' eccentricities; rotting gibbets still marking heinous crimes; mysterious posts identifying long forgotten ideas.

All of them remote, alone. Which, of course, is why we notice them, like houses on fenland or ships at sea. These are not the hidden curiosities of village or town. Their very isolation is an essential part of their history; whether deliberate – like a monumental eyecatcher, accidental – like the last remaining vestige of an abbey, or eminently practical – like a tunnel ventilator. All of them arousing curiosity, begging questions. Who hasn't wondered about that neo-Norman water tower by the M40 between Oxford and Banbury?

Many are in our peripheral vision on main roads: the tower in the trees between Oxford and Swindon at Faringdon, a Cold War jet fighter abandoned in a field next to the A1. And down the lesser known lanes it gets 'curiouser and curiouser' as we look around us at the fields and in the hedgerows. A faux steeple built on a Sussex horizon to win a bet for 'Mad Jack' Fuller. The Cross-and-Hand pillar where Thomas Hardy's Wessex comes to life on a lonely Dorset lane between Minterne Magna and Evershot. But not every curiosity comes with a neat tale or legend attached, many are highlighted here because they are simply incongruous in their surroundings or are even just neglected survivors from another age. But whatever and wherever they are, the English countryside will always amaze and intrigue those with a taste for these things, the characterful blips in the measured pulse of the landscape.

**Author's Note**

I have tried in most cases to record 'peculiars' that can be seen from a road, but of course it will be understood that their inclusion is not evidence of public access. Many will be on footpaths, but equally they may be on private land which should be respected or permission granted for taking a closer look. Therefore essential bits of kit in hunting them down will be the Ordnance Survey Explorer or Landranger maps (vital for plotting the now defunct triangulation pillars) and a pair of binoculars. I think it's also important to repeat the message from my little road safety book. I don't want to be nanny-ish about it, but please don't get distracted whilst driving by that Gothic tower on the left and always park sensibly and considerately on country lanes. And watch out for that herd of cows when you drive past Stonehenge.

ancient stones, lost ideas

### ROLLRIGHT, OXFORDSHIRE

A circle of eroded limestone monoliths sits in a grove of trees on a Cotswold ridge. These are the King's Men; their King sits behind railings on the other side of the road. Across a ploughed field the Whispering Knights lean on each other in mutual conspiracy. The story goes that they were all turned to stone by a witch, but this is probably untrue. What I find even stranger is that such things, usually more at home on Wiltshire downland or Scottish islands, are to be found here in the middle of Oxfordshire. The exact date of the stones' first appearance is as difficult to ascertain as they are apparently to count and I always feel slightly uneasy within their enclosure. There are the usual tales of individual stones being impossible to move successfully and I can well imagine the witch theory gaining a little more credence if one walked into the circle on a solitary moonless night.

The best time to come up here is on a winter's afternoon, when the smoke from the chimney of the little house where you pay your dues is drifting up into the bare branches of the trees. At this time of the year, there's more chance of being alone with your thoughts before succumbing to toasted teacakes down in Chipping Norton.

## MEN-AN-TOL, CORNWALL

In the mid-1970s my friends and I had many doubtful predilictions – and not just for impossibly flared trousers. We also devoured books like Alfred Watkin's *The Old Straight Track* (1925) and in particular the cosmic AA handbook, John Michell's *The View Over Atlantis* (1972). We got very carried away with megalithic science and ley lines and only stopped when someone pointed out that you can get straight lines by joining up telephone boxes if you try hard enough. But as the years roll past, revisiting these theorems and ideas is increasingly rewarding, none more so than when I visited the dolmens and menhirs of the Land's End peninsula.

Whilst normally praying for at least some sunlight, my visit to Men-an-tol coincided with an obliterating fog straight off the Atlantic, which only added to the sense of mystery. In this atmospheric setting the blackbirds silently perched on granite gateposts appeared very knowing but didn't let me into their secrets. Up a track between high stone walls and ditches sprouting red campion and purple foxgloves, this most curious of landmarks is finally found crouching low in the heather, three-quarters of a mile or so from the lane connecting Trevowhan with Madron.

In his *Popular Romances of the West of England* (1856),
Mr Robert Hunt says of the holed stone: 'If scrofulous
children are passed *naked* [his italics] through the Men-an-
tol three times, and then drawn on the grass three times
*against the sun*, it is felt by the faithful that much has been
done towards insuring a speedy cure.' In addition to
dragging shivering children about, crossed brass pins placed
on the stone would apparently answer questions with
peculiar movements like a 19th-century *Ask Jeeves*. The
point is, we actually have no idea what any of these stones
were for, but whatever it was they certainly still have the
power to move us in mysterious ways.

## LANYON QUOIT, CORNWALL

A little further on from Men-an-tol, but this time only just across a field from the lane, is Cornwall's trademark antiquity. It was once claimed that a man on horseback could ride under the capstone, but only a child could do so now without a scrape on the head. Opinion is divided about the reason for Lanyon Quoit; popularly it is reckoned to be the laid-bare internal framework for a chambered tomb, but apparently there is no evidence for this. Note my 'claimed', 'reckoned', 'apparently'. One needs safeguarding against infinitely more respectable knowledge, but I think all would agree to its unquestionable enigma. Dr Borlase, the local clergyman who studied the stones of Cornwall and published his findings in 1754, dug underneath it and found nothing to give any clue as to its purpose.

Lanyon Quoit has been much restored after falling down, once in a violent shipwrecking storm in 1815 when one of the supporting stones was broken. A Captain Giddy carried out a restoration with navy equipment in 1824 but had to shorten the remaining three supports, resulting in the considerable decrease in height. It is, of course, much visited, insensitively clambered over and overused as a backdrop for cagouled group photographs. Come here on a more solitary, fog-bound day and try to approach it on foot from at least a little distance away.

### HOLME, CAMBRIDGESHIRE

If stones could speak – and I imagine there are those who believe they can – what a tale these finely cut blocks would tell. They sit outside Engine Farm, a remote fenland farm east of Holme and, although they are just about visible from the road, it's best to ask permission to see them from the yard where forklifts shovel potatoes into lorries.

The Ordnance Survey map still marks this area as Whittlesey Mere and, until the mid-19th century, this was a vast stretch of original watery fen. It was the last such tract of land to be drained and as the water level dropped these stones emerged from the mud at the bottom. This is a land of black peaty soil that had never seen indigenous stone, so their appearance here was mystifying. Slowly it was revealed that they were stones cut in a quarry up on the stone belt – most likely north-east Northamptonshire – which were destined for the building of the abbey at either Ramsey or Sawtry. Watercourses were the arterial roads of their time and this was medieval England, so goods were carried down rivers and across meres on big flat-bottomed boats. Every now and then a boat would ground or capsize and the cargo would be jettisoned. And so these blocks of masonry never reached their destination, tumbling to rest in the black mud to be nudged by eels and pikes in the brackish gloom.

As they emerged they sat on the reclaimed farmland, with ploughmen working around them until finally a horse and cart was employed to carry them off to Engine Farm. The largest probably weighs a ton and careful inspection of the stones reveals the quarry mason's marks, the arrows and codes that are the medieval equivalent of 'This Way Up'.

## PRICKWILLOW, CAMBRIDGESHIRE

A path strikes out across the fen from Queen Adelaide on the edge of Ely. After a while it meets another track running west–east at an isolated tree that must be the successor of an original junction marker. Turning left we are on firmer ground, for this was the original Ely to Prickwillow road, superceded by a new road run out of Queen Adelaide in the 1930s. It is still a rough bridleway and on the left the chimneys of a house soon come into view poking up over tall green hedges.

This was once the Plough Inn, now a private house. Built into the fabric are large blocks of Barnack stone. In his mesmerising book *The Black Fens* (1957), A K Astbury says that this is another example of stone falling or being dropped out of a grounded boat, but the present owner of what is now called 'Old Plough' tells me he is of the view that the stone is indeed from Barnack, but in this case purloined when a sizeable chunk of Ely Cathedral fell down in the 15th century. He continually digs up these stone refugees in his garden.

certain markers, enduring pointers

### TRIANGULATION PILLARS

These are the standing stones of our age, hilltop markers plotting an invisible web of geometry, the oversize map pins of the mapmaker. And, in common with their megalithic forebears, they are now superseded by a newer, more advanced technology and are left neglected, forgotten and sometimes nudged and uprooted by farm machinery.

Taken for granted in their isolated positions, we perhaps forget just what an outstanding feat of human endeavour it was just to build them. Each tapering pillar is 4ft high on a 2ft square base and hand-cast in concrete. Easy enough, one might think. But what about getting the materials to the site? Many were obviously just about accessible by a tractor and trailer, but just a glance at the maps of hilly or mountainous country immediately evokes a completely different logistical problem. Imagine the effort involved in putting a trig point on Helvellyn in the Lake District or on Pen-y-ghent in the Yorkshire Dales.

Triangulation pillars were positioned on high ground so that a direct line could be established between them with a theodolite, a kind of telescopic compass that neatly slotted into the grooves on the bronze plate that sits on each pillar's top surface. This incredible network of over 6,000 pillars – constructed in the mid-1930s – was vital to the accurate mapping of the country and to the production of the new series of Ordnance Survey maps we still use and enjoy today. In-car satellite navigation systems and instructions sent to a mobile phone are really no substitute for the pleasure of reading a paper map flapping about on a windy hillside.

**Burrough Hill, Leicestershire** (*top left*)

**Wood's Corner, East Sussex** (*left*)

**Beacon Hill, Berkshire** (*top right*)

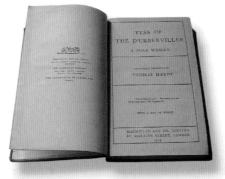

## BATCOMBE, DORSET *(left)*

A lonely road traverses a chalk ridge between Minterne Magna and Evershot. Above Batcombe a curious stone pillar sits in a hedgerow with the brambles and nettles. This amazing survivor is the Cross-and-Hand, probably either a Roman or Anglo-Saxon boundary marker. This pale stone has found a place in English literature and has subsequently become imbued with tales of murder, torture and, for good measure, a hanging.

If this sounds like something from the gloomy pen of Thomas Hardy you'd be right; he was so captured by its possibilities that he wrote about the pillar in both a poem, *The Lost Pyx*, and in his novel *Tess of the d'Urbervilles*. In the latter Hardy tells us: 'Of all spots on the bleached and desolate upland this was the most forlorn. It was so far removed from the charm which is sought in landscape by artists and view-lovers as to reach a new kind of beauty, a negative beauty of tragic tone.' Alex d'Urberville makes Tess place her hand upon it, telling her to swear she will never tempt him again.

Hardy's pal Sir Frederick Treves (he of Elephant Man fame) wrote of the stone in his *Highways and Byways in Dorset* (1906): 'It is a sort of Pillar of Salt in a place of hushed solitude, where are only gorse and heather and a never-tiring wind.'

## OAKLEY AND TURVEY, BEDFORDSHIRE

At the northern end of the parapet of Oakley Bridge over the Great Ouse is this curious limestone pillar *(top right)*. Closer inspection reveals it to be a marker to indicate the height of a great flood on 1 November 1823. When one stands next to it and looks around the surrounding countryside, one realises just what an exceptional flood this was.

The river navigates an impressive sequence of medieval and later bridges, and the spring flood water that surges up to the top of their arches still has the ability to competely change what one thought of as a familiar landscape, as at Turvey on the Bedfordshire/Buckinghamshire border *(right)*. The Great Ouse is one of our most substantial watercourses and before present-day relief schemes the river could render the entire broad valley completely unpassable in winter.

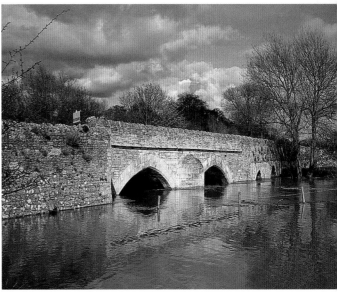

## BROUGHAM, CUMBRIA

You have to be very observant to catch a glimpse of the Countess Pillar. It sits up above the A66 on an embankment that separates the new road from the old road, where the pillar was erected in 1656. It can be found just to the east of Penrith and is one of those classic landmarks that children once looked out for as their Lake District holidays drew near.

Lady Anne Clifford of nearby Brougham Castle parted for the last time from her much-loved mother Margaret, Countess of Cumberland, at this spot on 2 April 1616; 40 years later she marked the location with this stone octagonal pillar. It is surmounted by a cube that has sundials on three sides. We owe much to Lady Anne Clifford, who was one of the first building conservationists, restoring to medieval splendour her family castles rather than modernising them: Skipton, Brough, Appleby, Pendragon and Brougham, which lies just to the west of the pillar. Her actions enraged Oliver Cromwell who had spent a not inconsiderable amount of time trying to blow up castles during the Civil War.

## ALCONBURY, CAMBRIDGESHIRE

The Old North Road and the Great North Road met at Alconbury for the big push northwards to York and over the border to Edinburgh. The junction was marked, and in an obscure way still is, by this beautiful milestone. Originally it was on a grassy triangle at the junction of the two coaching roads, but when I first saw this milestone it was in the middle of a dual carriageway surrounded by trees, a little to the north of the original site. Now it appears between the A1(M) and a service road, surrounded by low iron railings. All traces of the atmosphere of coaching days are now obliterated in motorway tarmac and acres of tin direction signs, but at least this symbol of travel in a quieter England still survives.

Alconbury Hill once struck a chilly note with coach passengers and drivers alike if travelling in winter. In this open country snow was likely to drift severely and on 31 January 1831 Francis Lord Jeffrey of Grantham wrote: 'Tonight it snows and blows, and there is good hope of our being blocked up at Witham Corner or Alconbury Hill, or some of these lonely retreats, for a week or so, or fairly stuck in the drifts.'

## ANDERSON, DORSET

This red signpost has been the source of much conjecture, even in the corridors of power at the local council who only comparatively recently learnt of the reason why they painted this particular signpost bright red. It all started in the 18th century, when if you weren't hung for a crime you stood a fair chance of being transported to a country so far away it might as well have been Mars. And if this was your fate and you were held in Dorchester Gaol then they further rubbed it in by making you walk to your ship in Portsmouth.

A day's march was around 14 miles, so as dusk approached the sorry band of prisoners and soldiers would have reached this spot on the road. It would have been rare for any of the party to be able to read, so the instructions were: 'Turn down the lane marked with a red signpost.' A few yards down this road was a building marked on the maps as Botany Bay Barn, named with grim humour after the likely destination in Australia. Here was the first overnight stop, the prisoners being chained up to a central wooden post. All it needed was for Thomas Hardy to write a story around it, which to my knowledge he never did, oddly enough.

## ALKBOROUGH, LINCOLNSHIRE

This is a bleak but quiet corner of England. Away from the roar of motorways but just to the north of industrial Scunthorpe, the village of Alkborough sits on top of a ridge called The Cliff, overlooking the flat marshland where the rivers Trent and Ouse meet to form the Humber. (Their joining can be seen in the background of the main photograph.) More East Yorkshire than Lincolnshire, it is a breathtaking landscape, a pattern of wide fields stretching out to the inland port of Goole and the minster at Howden.

In the village a path runs out from under the trees to a tiny field and here is slowly revealed, like a conjuring trick in the grass, a circular maze called Julian's Bower. Or is it a labyrinth? Apparently mazes lead you along frustrating paths to absolutely nowhere, whereas a labyrinth will eventually lead you to a crock of gold. Or a minotaur. I'll leave it to you to find out which Julian's is.

The Julian in this case is Julus, the son of Aeneas from the Troy saga in which mazes were something of an occupational hazard. Julus is credited with bringing maze games to Italy from Troy after its sacking by the Greeks. As with many of these curious figures cut into the landscape the Alkborough maze is difficult to date, although it is thought that monks from nearby Walcot probably had a hand in it. It is not difficult to see them up here, cowls pulled up against the wind as they worked, occasionally looking down the cliff to see big-sailed ships coming in with the tide from the open sea to waiting quaysides. An iron copy of the maze design is set into the floor of the parish church of St John the Baptist in Alkborough.

## FOVANT, WILTSHIRE

During the First World War Fovant, along with neighbouring villages Compton Chamberlayne and Sutton Mandeville, was a training and transit camp for the British Army. Thousands of soldiers – with their barracks, shooting ranges, a hospital and a camp cinema – filled the fields. There was even a branch railway to serve it, brought here off the main London to Exeter line.

Of course many soldiers never returned from the war and their comrades remembered them for posterity by carving the regimental cap badges into the downland chalk. Thirsty work on a 30 degree slope. By the end of that war there were 20 to be seen here, but by the Second World War the badges were left to grow over so that their presence would not give aid to enemy aircraft. Weather and cattle grazing added to their decay and the local Home Guard formed themselves into an Old Comrades Association, dedicated to restoring and preserving the badges. This in turn became The Fovant Badges Society, whose objectives are now being realised as the badges reappear on the grassy slopes, thanks to unstinting generosity from numerous benefactors. Sadly, for practical reasons some had to be allowed to gently fade away, but eight badges are still visible (five of which are seen above). To further protect them, viewing is restricted to a lay-by on the A30 Salisbury to Shaftesbury road, but at least there is a very well designed information board that admirably aids the identification of the individual badges.

## UFFINGTON, OXFORDSHIRE

This beautifully abstract horse is very likely our oldest chalk figure. There are other white horses cut out of the chalk of English downland, with more traditional animals at Cherhill and Westbury and one with King George III in uniform on its back near Osmington in Dorset, but here above Uffington is the most lively and enigmatic. The hill itself is the highest point in Oxfordshire at 857ft.

Its clearly defined lines are owed to regular repair, or 'scouring', where the turf is trimmed back and new chalk added to the design. These scourings were once great celebratory events when local villagers would have gathered up here in the hundreds. But perhaps the most remarkable thing about this horse is that it is impossible to get the complete picture from either the hill or indeed the surrounding countryside. It can be seen in its entirety from afar, but only as a distorted flattened image. The only way it fully reveals itself is from the air, so you can imagine the arguments that get put forward as to its use. I couldn't run to a helicopter to show you the full effect (one did clatter overhead on my visit with a photographer hanging out of it, just to taunt me) so I have included the covers of R Hippisley Cox's seminal work *The Green Roads of England* (1934) and that of a Murray's Architectural Guide (1949) that proves the White Horse has galloped abstractedly all the way from Berkshire.

## CERNE ABBAS, DORSET

*Discussing a chalk giant with a thirty-foot erection was not considered good after-dinner conversation, however true it might have been.*

Julian Cope *The Modern Antiquarian* (1998)

The chronology of this 180ft giant is difficult to pin down and the more we try to date figures like this the more they appear to age or grow younger by thousands of years. But the real trouble with this giant has always been his penis. Or rather people's reaction to it. Over the centuries the member for Mid-Dorset has been a centre of ritual, with childless women communing with it and conceptions initiated on it, but equally it has frequently been covered up like a censor's black bar over an explicit photograph.

You can just imagine what the Victorians thought about it, with distraught clergy refusing to condone his cleaning in 1868 in order to protect the morals of their flocks. Even books in the early 20th century had the penis rendered as a vague collection of fine dots. The Women's Institute was ever practical, however, recommending that pregnancy could be advanced by drinking from St Augustine's Well in the churchyard down in Cerne Abbas, using a cup made out of a laurel leaf, facing the church but presenting one's back to the giant.

Most scholars agree that this aggressive sexual display is a representation of Hercules, but confusion is rife about his date because the first documented reference to him was made in 1759 and no mention of him appears in the very comprehensive medieval manuscripts for Cerne Abbas. There is even one school of thought that makes him a piece of vicious Cromwellian satire, a kind of Gerald Scarfe cartoon in chalk but with a long-lost caption. Whatever his origins, we should enjoy him as he is, even if on my visit he did look as if a good scouring wouldn't be amiss.

## BRIDGWATER, SOMERSET

This superb figure runs energetically south with outstretched arms, through a field at the side of the M5 between Junctions 24 and 23. He is made from willow, a crop of the nearby Somerset Levels, and was sculpted by Serena de la Hey. The outer skin of willow is interwoven over a steel skeleton and, since the first Willow Man on the site was burnt down in May 2001, he is reinforced with steel threads.

### NORTHAMPTONSHIRE SCARECROWS

Scarecrows in the popular imagination are probably of the straw-filled Worzel Gummidge variety. These days you are most likely to see them in a Scarecrow Festival. This watchful example (*left*) was hung on a signpost for the Aldwincle festival, where scarecrows have also been posed in the church for a scarecrow wedding, hung out of upstairs windows as house burglars and even strewn over the local garage forecourt in a ghastly tableau of a particularly nasty road accident.

Out in the fields the scarecrow has now largely been made redundant by deafening explosions from gas canisters, but now and then a strange figure appears in the landscape and we find the tradition still alive and well, if not wildly effective. I found this abstracted Rupert Bear (*above*) in a field at the side of the bridleway where horses were once led over the top of the Braunston canal tunnel.

Blatherwycke is as strange as it sounds. Open country surrounds the remnants of parkland that once served the Hall, which was demolished after suffering terrible deprivations at the hands of billeted soldiers in the Second World War. There is still a gate lodge, stables and a hidden church with a Norman tower, but everything here is an echo of past lives, of past greatness. If you follow the footpath to King's Cliffe that skims the edge of the park, you will see this strange apparition (*above and right*) on the horizon. A stone statue so out of context amongst the crops that questions crowd in more easily than the answers. It is, simply, a garden ornament moved from the grounds of the Hall to stand on the ridge, a scarecrow Adonis whether or not that was the intention. He is now very weather-beaten, his right leg peeling away to reveal an iron armature, a classical bionic muscle.

private crimes, public punishments

### COMBE, BERKSHIRE

Combe Gibbet stands unnervingly high above a long barrow burial mound that possibly dates from 3500 BC. It is reached up a bridleway cutting across the chalk between Inkpen Beacon and Walbury Hill, at a point where it is difficult to know whether one is in Wiltshire, Berkshire or Hampshire, for they all meet up here.

The gibbet was first erected to display the executed bodies of George Broomham and his mistress Dorothy Newman. They were convicted of the brutal and callous murder of Broomham's wife and son, one version of the tale relishing the spectacle of the wife being thrown into a hornet's nest in a nearby chalk pit. There was much wrangling amongst local villages as to who should stump up the cash for the gibbet, but finally (did they throw a dice?) Combe was elected to provide it. Such was its importance as a landmark it was judged that when the gibbet was struck by lightning or suffered at the hands of vandals it should be replaced. The tenancy of a local farm still has in its agreement that the cost should be born by the incumbents. Writing in 1940 Edmund Vale noted in his *Curiosities of Town and Countryside* that the gibbet at that time was the third to be erected here.

Gibbeted corpses were often given a coat of tar and hung up in chains or encased in an iron frame which was attached to the skull by the simple expedient of having a screw twisted into it. Gruesome scarecrows indeed, swinging sullenly in the downland breeze, rusty iron coats grating softly.

## CAXTON, CAMBRIDGESHIRE (*left*)

Drive along the undulating miles of the A1198 between Royston and Huntingdon late on a summer's evening and it is very easy to imagine a highwayman lurking in a spinney or an ostler shading his eyes outside a coaching inn. North of Caxton the road burrows through dark trees up to a crossroads where this gibbet stands silhouetted against the sky. To the right is Cambridge, to the left St Neots, and an inn (now a Chinese restaurant), which was once the staging post for the former. So this was a good place for gibbeting, the practice of displaying corpses at a location other than at the place of execution. A welcome sight then for travellers tired from the long coach haul up from London, looking forward to roaring fires, beefsteak pies and being attended to by rosy-cheeked servants, only to have a goggle-eyed cadaver stare through the window as an aperitif.

There are many stories connected to the Caxton Gibbet, including that of a murderer hung up and starved to death in the iron cage that was the gibbet's main accessory and that of three fellows accused of sheep stealing who are buried underneath. The last felon to swing here was the son of a local landlord who murdered three of his father's guests and hid their bodies in a well under the inn stairs. Although now a replica, the timbers at least come from a contemporary local but demolished cottage, probably one of vernacular A-frame construction.

## BILSTONE, LEICESTERSHIRE (*right*)

Many of the gallows and gibbets we see today tend to be reproductions erected on the same spot as their gruesome originals, but I am fairly confident that this stump in a hedgerow near Bilstone is the real thing. From the top section, now rotted away, the corpse of John Massey was hung in chains, a murderer who had been executed earlier at Red Hill near Leicester on 23 March 1801. As was the custom, his body was displayed here as a warning to others, on a public road as near to the scene of the crime as possible.

Massey was a man 'punctual in dealing and industrious in business but much addicted to passion'. This passion saw him kick his wife into a mill stream that ran a quarter of a mile away across a field beside the Bilstone to Congerstone road. She died seven weeks later. Massey's 10-year-old stepdaughter witnessed his crime and later gave the damning evidence that sent him to the gallows.

His execution aroused great interest because in his younger days Massey was a notoriously agile wrestler who threw his opponents over his head, earning him the sobriquet Topsy Turvy. His carrion-pecked corpse stayed hanging at this spot for the next 17 years. In fact Massey had requested this rather than have his remains end up on a trainee surgeon's table. Eventually the whole gruesome business of gibbeting came to an end in 1834.

## LISKEARD, CORNWALL

One of the most outstanding engineering feats of past times was without doubt the construction of the Great Western Railway from London to Penzance. Under the shrewd and masterful eye of Isambard Kingdom Brunel cuttings were dug, embankments raised, stations built and locomotives constructed. Dramatic bridges spanned the Thames at Maidenhead and the Tamar at Saltash. And in Cornwall viaducts leapt over deep cut valleys and muddy tidal creeks. Many had wooden trackways supported by stone piers; others were entirely constructed in wood. One of the former wood and stone constructions crossed the Looe River to the west of Liskeard at Moorswater.

This was one of the most spectacular of the Cornish viaducts, striding high across the valley on 14 stone piers. Two collapsed during construction, so Brunel went for a belt and braces approach with much sparring and strutting to support his 7ft broad gauge single track. To travel over it at speed was an alarming event, much commented on in the press. One can imagine the noisy combination of creaking and vibrating being very unsettling; passengers must have put their heads in their laps, braced like the emergency diagrams you look at on aircraft.

It all got too much eventually and the viaduct was replaced in 1881. But six piers and the stumps of a further four survive, stone giants standing like arched towers next to their successors. They can be seen from the A38 streaming above, but for a closer look you must navigate around a little industrial estate in the valley on a dark lane that winds down to Coombe station on the Liskeard to Looe branch line, a delightful pleasure in itself.

## FAZELEY, STAFFORDSHIRE

Canal bridges are usually red brick humps out in the fields or decorative cast-iron arches sweeping over junctions. Sometimes the presence of a country house near a projected canal would see the landowner demanding something out of the ordinary and I imagine that's what happened here on the Birmingham & Fazeley Canal. Very close to the entrance to Drayton Manor, this is essentially a swing-bridge with a footbridge in attendance. What makes it so unique are the two white-painted crenallated towers that house the spiral staircases that go up to the wooden walkway over the canal.

## HOVINGHAM, NORTH YORKSHIRE

Alone in a North Yorkshire field, this bridge is of such
pretensions that one is immediately surprised that it is so
isolated and without the customary landscaping associated
with its time. It was not always so.

Thomas Worsley, Surveyor-General of the King's Works,
inherited the estate from his father, also Thomas, in 1751.
Landscaping was well underway and as Thomas started
building the present hall he directed his passion for
gardening into forming a lake from his father's garden canal.
It culminated in this Palladian bridge built in 1771–2 at a
cost of £145 12s 2½d. In the 19th century the lake was
abandoned in favour of a canal again and at this point the
cascade immediately in front of the bridge was created.
In time even this water course reverted back to the tiny
stream that we see today meandering through the pasture,
leaving the bridge quite literally high and nearly dry.

But times often come full circle and over the last 20 years
there has been much replanting at Hovingham Hall and,
as a result, it has started to recover the look and
atmosphere of the original 18th-century parkland.

## IFORD MANOR, WILTSHIRE

The bridge at Iford Manor that crosses over the Frome is not strictly pastoral, but it is as
remote as it is beautiful. Immersed in a wooded valley to the south-west of Bradford-on-Avon,
the manor is only just in Wiltshire, as difficult to find on a map as it is to find in reality. The
house is of the early 18th century, pale gold stone against a hillside of dark trees. The gardens
were landscaped by Harold Peto in the 1900s, an eccentric, lively, funny architect who brought
an Italian cascade of terraces, loggias and balustrades to the banks of the tumbling Frome. Peto
was in partnership with Ernest George and they gave us an appetizing butcher's shop in Mayfair
that has lots of dusty pink terracotta details and game from the Home Counties hanging up
outside. A young Edwin Lutyens cut his teeth in the practice and was much influenced by Peto.

Across the lane from the house is a 15th-century bridge gracefully arching over the rushing
water and on the parapet is a figure that never fails to capture the imagination. Peto put
the lichen-covered Britannia statue here, perhaps in order to listen to the spirits of the river.
I always think it looks like an outcast from a roofline in 18th-century Bath.

## SEATON, RUTLAND

This colossus of railway engineering spans the Welland valley between the villages of Seaton in Rutland and Harringworth in Northamptonshire. The river that flows under it forms the county boundary. I seem to remember that an annual tug-of-war between the two parishes was once held here, with the winner claiming the right for the viaduct to take their village name for a year. There is also conjecture about whether its 82 arches (each costing £1,000) are constructed of red brick patched with blue or blue brick patched with red. Well, until someone has a tug-of-war with me over it, it was originally built in blue engineering bricks in 1879 and, at 1,275 yards, it is the longest viaduct in the country outside of London. Over a million sheepskins were laid down to help drain the waterlogged meadows. The photograph (*above*) shows that the water regularly reclaims its ground: these are January floods giving the illusion of an estuarine landscape.

### TYRINGHAM, BUCKINGHAMSHIRE

Any mental list of architects will always have certain names underscored heavily with a metaphorical draughtsman's pen to denote their pre-eminence: Inigo Jones, John Vanbrugh, Christopher Wren. My own underlining would probably finish off with Edwin Lutyens and Charles Voysey. And then there's John Soane (1753–1837), who is as near a genius as it gets in architectural terms. His buildings are described in the *Penguin Dictionary of Architecture* as 'intense, severe, and sometimes affectedly odd … reflect[ing] his tricky character'.

If you turn off the Northampton to Newport Pagnell road for Tyringham House you will go through a gateway that is indeed intense and severe, and then you will rise up over a humpbacked bridge over the Great Ouse as it winds through the park. Both the gateway and bridge have Soane's signatures of finely incised lines and round-headed alcoves, giving us a good idea of his very personal style. They are two survivors because in 1909 the late 18th-century house behind the trees was completely, and some would say tastelessly, altered. Take time to have a proper look at this elegant bridge alone in the fields; there is something emphatically powerful about it and yes, a very Soanian sense of being 'affectedly odd'.

### ROTHERHAM, SOUTH YORKSHIRE

Keppel's Pillar once stood alone on the Wentworth Woodhouse estate, but the encroachment of Rotherham now means that it stands sentinel over a little housing estate to the north-west of the town. It is of an age when landowners could express themselves and their opinions in a myriad of ways, the folly being the most prominent and sometimes the most self-obsessed. But when he was asked about this blackened chimney of 1782, the Marquis of Rockingham bucked the trend by telling his audience that he erected it in order to proclaim his trust in a friend.

Admiral Keppel was court martialled after the Battle of Ushant in 1778 by corrupt politicians who desperately needed a scapegoat in order to hide the fact that they had trousered the money Keppel needed to repair his fleet of ships. Rockingham did what we'd all do if confronted by a friend in need and ran out and built a Doric column on his estate. The sooty pillar can be found on the A629 between Rotherham and Chapeltown.

### NORTHAMPTON, NORTHAMPTONSHIRE

An isolated chimney can be found in a scruffy field to the south-east of the town. A quick look round the base would indicate that it was never attached to a building, on the surface at least, but next door is a waterworks that probably provides a clue to an answer that has so far escaped me. However, the chimney is peculiar and does provide an effective use of two local varieties of stone, much appreciated by the dogs taking their recreation in the semi-rural park in which it stands.

### DEENE PARK, NORTHAMPTONSHIRE

At first sight this appears to be a straightforward obelisk in a country park. Erected in celebration of the turn of the millennium, this is a classic tapering column in the local limestone. It is aligned with the main entrance of Deene Park, the ancestral home of the Brudenells who number in their august forebears Lord Cardigan, the 'Homicidal Earl' who led the heroic, if ill-fated, Charge of the Light Brigade. Closer inspection, however, reveals an eccentric finishing touch crowning the top of the column, a beautifully proportioned stone teapot pointing its spout hopefully back at the house where presumably stone cups and saucers are waiting.

I am reliably informed that tea is the favourite beverage of the present occupier of Deene Park, which gave rise to a discussion with my informant about which refresher we would have placed on our own obelisks. She went for a large glass of chilled white wine, me for a carefully balanced grouping of pints of Bass. The conversation came to a close when we wondered if anyone would choose a mug of Bournvita.

### PORTESHAM, DORSET

Dorset celebrates two Thomas Hardys. Were they by any chance related? This fat dumb-bell of a tower celebrates Thomas Masterman Hardy who spent his boyhood down in the village of Portesham below. He was the friend and embracer of Admiral Nelson, who fell on the ship under his command at the Battle of Trafalgar, the fortuitously named *HMS Victory*. Nelson almost certainly did say 'Kiss me Hardy' and not 'Kismet Hardy' as those who shrink from such things would have us believe, and he didn't wear an eyepatch either. That was Laurence Olivier in *That Hamilton Woman*.

Appropriately Hardy's Monument looks out over the sea, notably the extraordinary Chesil Beach and the Isle of Portland. They say that if you can see the grey stack from a distance it's going to rain. In my experience if you can't see it, it's already bucketing down. Designed by Arthur Dyke Acland-Troyte the monument stands 70ft high and was erected by public subscription in 1844. There is a spiral staircase inside to the top, where one can be rewarded by expansive views like this one of an approaching storm.

Hardy always held Portesham close to his heart, sending messages to the beloved 'Possum' of his boyhood to enquire after consignments of Dorset ale. And there is a connection to the other Hardy. In 1938 a sale was held of author Thomas Hardy's effects and an engraved portrait of Admiral Hardy fetched nine shillings.

## SOUTH KYME, LINCOLNSHIRE

Lincolnshire is one of my favourite counties. Little visited (there are no motorways) unless quickly passed through on Wold or marshland roads to the irredeemably flat but atmospheric coastline, the county can always be guaranteed to show something unexpected. All you need to do is take off down the byroads. It may be forgotten delights like a little church tucked into a fold of the Wolds at Oxcombe or a timber cinema in a wood at Woodhall Spa. Or the names: Mavis Enderby, Candlesby, Hannah-cum-Hagnaby. And always something slightly odd, like this tower at South Kyme.

The tower is the only surviving fragment of a house built in the 14th century by Sir Gilbert de Umfraville. It has four storeys with a stair turret bringing the height to 77ft. The house was dismantled in the early 18th century, leaving this ashlar-faced reminder alone in a field surrounded by quietly sighing chestnuts and sycamores.

### BRADGATE PARK, LEICESTERSHIRE

Bradgate Park is an uncultivated tract of rock-strewn country surrounding a Tudor mansion whose ruins lie at its heart. One of the earliest unfortified houses in England, the red brick house was once the home of Lady Jane Grey, the nine days Queen who lost her head to the ruthless political manoeverings of the age. Tradition has it that all the parkland oaks were pollarded in her memory, trees that are still in evidence today. The park itself has never been landscaped and is therefore an extremely rare example of how a medieval hunting ground would have looked. The whole is surrounded by a stone wall 4½ miles long.

Deer still graze under the trees and to the north-west of the ruins this little tower sits on its outcrop of igneous rock. A windmill was converted by the 5th Earl of Stamford in 1786 to form this memorial to Old John, an aged retainer. Old John was the miller and met his end when either a tree or flagpole at the heart of a celebratory bonfire made with faggots and barrels of tar fell on him. Leicestershire in the 18th century was not unduly exercised with obtrusive health and safety measures.

Old John would have been used as a prospect tower to follow hunts and when the Quorn met in the park the tower came into its own as a refreshment stop. At 700ft the hill is the highest point of the park, commanding breathtaking views over the surrounding countryside. The 828 acres were given to the people of Leicester and Leicestershire by Charles Bennion in 1928, a unique and beautiful playground for children and adults alike, within easy reach of the city.

LEICESTERSHIRE
RAMBLERS
FEDERATION

## BROADWAY, WORCESTERSHIRE

All hilltop towers claim impressive prospects. 'From up here,' they say, 'you can see seven counties.' But does the Broadway Tower pass muster with James Lees-Milne's claim of 13? It only just sneaks into Worcestershire, so we can immediately take two counties for granted, the other being Gloucestershire. Warwickshire, Northamptonshire, Oxfordshire, Monmouthshire and Herefordshire should be possible; Wiltshire and Buckinghamshire are pushing it a bit. That still leaves four more to go. On an exceptionally clear day I expect you might get bits of Berkshire, Leicestershire and Shropshire. And I suppose the pale mauve hills on the far western horizon give us Powys. The thing is, how do we know? I've never been anywhere in south-west Leicestershire and thought 'Oh look! Broadway Tower!' Of course, the exercise, even if totally academic, is still fun to think about when you're on top of this 1,024ft high hill.

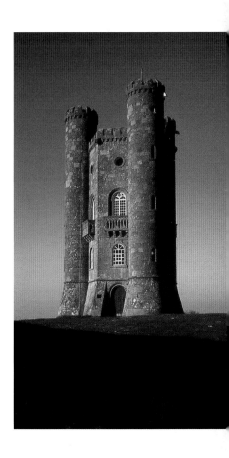

The beautifully preserved tower was built in 1797 by George William, 6th Earl of Coventry, to improve the view from his home at Croome Court to the west of Pershore. The countess insisted that a beacon was lit on the hill to ensure that it could indeed be seen from the house. She was right to. Only 14 miles or so divide them, but a crow's flightline between the two locations goes straight through Bredon Hill. The designer was James Wyatt, who brought together all the fashionable details of Norman round-headed windows, turrets, machicolation and battlements. The tower is open all the year round and can be found above the Cotswold town of Broadway in a country park.

### HORTON, DORSET

In the 1760s Humphrey Sturt played with the idea of putting an observatory up here in order to watch the heavens over east Dorset, but it is far more likely that foxes and their pursuing hunts were more closely observed than interstellar movement. I don't think this broad-shouldered giant needed to have a purpose particularly. Who wouldn't get pleasure just from looking at the 6-storey hexagon with its three-quarter-round turrets topped-out by mustard pot lids?

In 1967 a few lengths of Technicolor movie frames showed off Horton Tower to the world. It was used as the location for the illicit cockfight in John Schlesinger's epic film *Far from the Madding Crowd*, the scene where Sergeant Troy gets taken to the cleaners by a smug bowler-hatted member of the gentry. The tower provided a grim accusing silhouette with horses and carriages waiting outside for the outcome of the bloody squawking and crowing echoing within its tall brick walls.

But one of the best stories is probably the most recent. Many hilltop towers get enrolled into service as convenient places to string up mobile phone antennae and Horton was an obvious candidate. Except that here someone gave it a bit of thought and the transmitting gubbins are very cleverly disguised as part of the fabric. You can discern them on the faces of the hexagonal top portion, cleverly painted rectangles that are easily absorbed into the character of the tower. And so Horton Tower does at last reach out to the stars, finally achieving a practical purpose after 240 years of dominating the surrounding countryside.

### FARINGDON, OXFORDSHIRE

Lord Berners was one of the most brilliant stars in the firmament of English eccentrics. He had a clavichord in the back of his Rolls-Royce, dyed fantail doves in rainbow colours and when playing the piano supplemented his hands with his bottom. He was the model for Lord Merlin in Nancy Mitford's *The Pursuit of Love*.

A man like this had to have a folly built and one duly arrived on a hill above Faringdon in 1935, possibly the last of its kind. His great friends John and Penelope Betjeman were at the opening. It sits on Folly Hill, a landmark on the Oxford to Swindon road that only just rises above a dark wood where foxgloves can also be seen reaching up to the light. At Christmas time a bright star is lit at the top.

Lord Berners wanted the Gothic style and was not pleased when he returned from Rome to find that his architect, Lord Gerald Wellesley, had gone for a classical tower. A Gothic top was subsequently added. All involved hoped for apoplectic outrage from the locals and this was very swift in coming. A Miss Lobb complained, amongst other things, that the new tower was an invitation to would-be suicides. Berners promptly nailed up a notice: 'All persons wishing to commit suicide do so at their own risk.'

He was also an artist – memorably designing the cover for the first *Shell Guide* to Wiltshire – and painted his folly on its tree-topped hill for a Shell poster that was pasted-up on the sides of the lorries used for delivering cans of petrol and oil.

### BALDERTON, NOTTINGHAMSHIRE

The imagination can run riot here at Balderton. This tower, of such overpoweringly surreal proportions and colour, looks dark and sinister even on a cloudless day. Backlit against a raging sunset it could provide an illustration for a rural outpost of the Ministry of Truth in *Nineteen Eighty-Four* or a hellish image for a Dracula movie set in the 1930s.

In thankful reality it's a chimney, which served the Balderton Hospital that once gathered at its feet. The structure is part of a hospital development that was started in 1936. Wartime halted construction and the large Victorian house on the site was used by officers from Balderton airfield. Work recommenced in 1945, but it was not finally opened until 1957 by Enoch Powell, the Minister for Health. It was a mental hospital, and the sunnier of these two pictures shows the laundry, which in itself is an indicator of how extensive the operation was here. The hospital has vanished, closed in 1993, though the chimney remains. It is now surrounded by an estate of 'executive' houses in the usual pastiche of styles.

## CHESTERTON, WARWICKSHIRE

When I first saw this curious structure it had no sails and I suppose it looked then much as it was first built in 1632 as an observatory. These fields are part of the lost estate of Sir Edward Peto, who very likely designed the building, although, like many others of doubtful provenance, it is often attributed to Inigo Jones.

We don't know exactly when it was converted to a windmill, but we do know that new machinery was installed in 1860. It was last used as a working mill in 1910. With its elephantine stance it seems a very impractical building to convert into a windmill, and missing now is the timber structure that sat between the arches, which contained the staircase and a lower bay for the hoist. As with tower mills the cap is revolved by internal gearing so that the sails can be moved into the wind.

Up until the 1930s the field below the mill was used as a point-to-point course and the disused mill made an excellent grandstand for watching the Warwickshire hunts. One can imagine the shouts of encouragement from folk in battered trilbys standing on the roofs of equally battered station wagons corralled around the mill, but all is quiet here now.

puzzling follies, prodigious expenses

## DALLINGTON, EAST SUSSEX

'Mad Jack' Fuller MP was one of those genial eccentrics that the popular early 19th-century press probably illustrated as a bucolic John Bull. Weighing 20 stone, unmarried and benefiting from the wealth of the Sussex iron industry, Jack Fuller indulged himself in many passions, not the least of which was building follies on his estate at Brightling. These included an obelisk, a hermit's tower and an observatory. The wall around the park was built just to provide employment and 24 years before his death he designed and built a pyramid in Brightling churchyard to contain his remains. Rumours persisted for years that he was interred sitting upright at a table with a bottle of port and a roasted bird, but subsequent renovation of the tomb immediately disproved the story, more's the pity. One suspects that Jack Fuller put the story about just to get everybody going, not least the vicar of Brightling with whom he had enjoyed numerous run-ins.

Fuller liked his drink and during a session with his London pals he claimed that Dallington church spire could be seen from his home. On the comment being vigorously disputed he entered into a not inconsiderable wager. On his return he discovered his boast was erroneous in the extreme, Dallington church being in a dip below the horizon. He quickly marshalled his workforce and built this stone and cement sugar loaf in a field just off the Battle to Heathfield road at Wood's Corner. The bet was presumably either won or Fuller was found out, but either way the interior was later used as a cottage. However, with a blind window and no chimney, one assumes the cottage's occupant was an ascetic with little regard for home comforts.

Comparison with the real spire (*right*) can be made by visiting St Giles church in the village of Dallington, three-quarters of a mile to the south-west.

## WATLINGTON, OXFORDSHIRE

Here on a hot Chiltern hillside there is a slender triangle cut into the short-cropped turf. This is the Watlington White Mark and once again a story is told of a faux spire that pretends to be where it isn't. Apparently in 1764 local squire Edward Horne thought that Watlington church would look better if it had a spire. A labour force was soon put to work cutting out the chalk to create a 270ft high illusion, so that from his home it aligned with the top of the tower of St Leonard's. Apart from the immense amount of semaphore flag waving and messengers sweating up the steep hillside to say 'Down a bit your side, Nathaniel', the idea doesn't appear to work wherever you are, and if you do manage to more or less line it all up by squatting in a field with your head between your legs the triangle still leans vertiginously to the right. Of course now I expect to hear that if you stand on the upstairs lavatory seat at 55 Acacia Avenue and look out of the window the effect is complete.

The idea is so English I suppose it could just be true, but the *Victoria County History* and many subsequent accounts merely say that this is a representation in chalk of a giant obelisk. It could be that nobody believed that an 18th-century squire could be barmy enough to go to so much trouble, but as we can see in this book it really is perfectly possible.

## COMPTON WYNYATES, WARWICKSHIRE

Compton Wynyates is one of the most romantic houses in England and is achingly beautiful in both its building and setting. It was once open to the public, but sadly no more. However, up on top of a field opposite the house is this slender pyramid with a bobble on top. This is Compton Pike, a curious name that suggests something you'd find on a vigorous hike in the North Country rather than in a Warwickshire field. Most sources claim it's one of the 16th-century beacons used to frighten the population into thinking the Armada had invaded, but that does raise the query as to why it looks like this. I thought beacons were iron cages on poles, or at least a hearth of some kind, so I would like to think it's a true folly, put here just for the hell of it.

## FARLEY DOWN, HAMPSHIRE

This rare monument to a sporting horse – a white 30ft high pyramid with a yew tree at each corner of its mound – can be found up on the downs to the west of Winchester. Underneath is buried a horse that, whilst out hunting in September 1733, fell into a 25ft deep chalk pit and survived. The animal's rider, Mr Paulet St John, then entered the horse into the Hunter's Plate race on Worthy Down the following year and won it. He had renamed his steed 'Beware Chalk Pit'.

The pyramid is now part of a Hampshire country park, with wide-ranging views over towards Winchester and Portsmouth. Two identical iron plates attached to it tell us in clear embossed letters that it was restored in 1870 by the Rt Hon Sir William Heathcote Baronet.

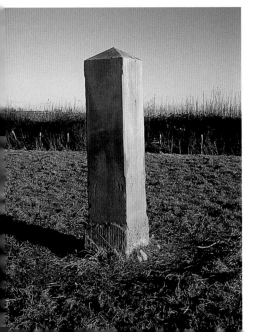

## EAST LANGTON, LEICESTERSHIRE

Another horse memorial is found stuck out in the middle of a field on a footpath to the south of East Langton. This simple stone looks more like a stray gate pier or a cattle rubbing post, for which purpose it is doubtless used. It commemorates the passing of a horse called Lottery on 21 February 1886. One wonders if the animal's bloodline stretched back to the winner of the first Grand National in 1839, also named Lottery.

## BARWICK, SOMERSET

The weather in late June was perfect for folly hunting. A thunderstorm
had threatened in the west all morning, the skies becoming ever deeper
shades of ink blue before finally erupting with apocalyptic ferociousness.
As I crept through a cloudburst around Yeovil I finally found a deep lane
that I hoped would lead to Barwick. It tunnelled down through dark yellow
cliffs of stone, emerging out into fields where to my relief I saw my quarry,
theatrically lit by lightning a quarter of a mile away. As it grew brighter I
found a footpath where I had to shoulder towering rain-drenched stalks
of giant hogweed out of my way. Suddenly, there he was, a naked Mercury
balancing on his pinnacle up in the trees, staring down on my sodden
figure below.

We know little about the Barwick Park follies, but four out of five mark the
main points of the compass on the boundaries of the estate. They were
probably built by George Messiter and, equally vaguely, were possibly
constructed to provide employment during a depression in Yeovil's glove
trade in the 1820s. The best of all of them is Jack the Treacle Eater.

Jack was one of the fastest runners in England at the time and his speed
was used by the Messiters for taking messages up to London. To maintain
his strength he filled himself up with treacle. One assumes he was greatly
loved if this is his memorial, a rough stone arch with tower and tiptoe
mascot. Another story is that the little tower room was used as a refuge
for a murderer whose mother secretly brought him treacle to sustain his
sojourn. Locals will tell you that if you leave treacle at the bottom of the
tower it will have been devoured by Jack during the night.

### MIDDLETON STONEY, OXFORDSHIRE

For some reason the M40 motorway between Oxford and Banbury is noticeably bereft of landmarks to mark your journey. The one major exception is this neo-Norman water tower, in a field on the left as you approach Junction 10 (on a northbound journey). We need markers like these to highlight our progressions, something to watch out for to keep us on our toes. Think of the impact of the Angel of the North, Antony Gormley's stunning steel giant spreading out his aircraft wings above Gateshead on the A1, or Serena de la Hey's striding Willow Man (see p 33) on the M5 at Bridgwater.

This is only a simple water tower, once isolated in a field but now presiding over six lanes of thundering traffic. But someone had the idea of placing the tank on graceful arches, roofing it in a very French style and adding the modernist touch of a radial-cornered walkway. The sides of the tower have the arches repeated as blind arcading and at its base is a secondary entrance archway built in a rough rustic style. The tower can be reached by a footpath that dips off a lane running between Bucknell and Middleton Stoney, well-known by anglers who trudge down it to angle about in Trow Pool.

### WEST NEWTON, NORFOLK (top left)

The Appleton Water Tower serviced the royal estate of Sandringham. Both the Prince of Wales (the future Edward VII) and his eldest son had fallen sick with typhoid, so this tower is very likely part of an attempt to improve the quality of the water at the house. Designed by Martin Ffolkes, this extraordinary tower was started in July 1877, immediately resulting in a 'Right Royal Row' between the Prince of Wales and a tenant farmer over damage caused by construction traffic.

The ground and first floors of the carstone octagon were used by the caretaker as his living accommodation and the second floor was used as a convenient viewing platform by royal parties. Often this type of tower would have enclosed the water tank itself, but here it is fully displayed and painted red just in case there could be any doubt as to the tower's purpose. The caretaker's homely fires kept the water from freezing in winter. You can experience living here for yourself as the Appleton Water Tower is now in the care of the inestimable Landmark Trust.

### RAVENSDEN, BEDFORDSHIRE (top centre)

Some people feel that many water towers are merely white-painted concrete blots on the landscape. Here in eastern England they are often the only thing in the landscape. Water towers are necessary where the gradients of hills are insufficient to maintain a good head of water and, like all things, the acceptability of their presence in isolated countryside comes down to design. The 120ft high Ravensden tower on a bend of the B660 between Bedford and Kimbolton works particularly well. The elegantly tapering side walls have sets of neat square windows on alternate sides, spaced out between pilasters that rise up dramatically to finally splay out to support the tank. Another designer might have castellated the top edge in faux medievalism, but the restraint here is admirable. You probably wouldn't want it looking over your back garden, but here, soaring over the quiet arable fields, it is a true landmark in the very best sense of the word.

### MAPPLETON, EAST YORKSHIRE (top right)

Wellsian science fiction can be found out on the plains of Holderness. The water tower at Mappleton is the only one of this design I've come across and it's as if the water company's draughtsman got bored one Friday afternoon and thought 'Hmmm, I know…'

## PYLONS

*Now over those small hills*          *But far above and far*
*they built the concrete*             *as sight endures*
*that trails black wire*              *Like whips of anger*
*Pylons those pillars*               *With lightning's danger*
*Bare like nude, giant girls*         *There runs the quick*
*that have no secret*                 *perspective of the future.*

Stephen Spender *The Pylons* (1933)

If you had to design a tower to carry 400,000 volts worth of electricity about the countryside, the pylon as we see it here in rural Lincolnshire is not a bad solution. Even at the start of the National Grid in 1933 there were sensibilities about the impact of such things and they brought in Sir Reginald Blomfield to look at the design possibilities. Blomfield had been on the Royal Fine Arts Commission that had chosen Giles Gilbert Scott's design for the red telephone box, and Scott, architect of Liverpool Cathedral and Battersea Power Station, has always been associated with the pylon project.

There is continual controversy about overhead wires, but there are also environmental implications for stuffing them underground, quite apart from practical considerations. On our National Grid there are over 22,000 of these galvanised steel giants in England and Wales, around six per mile by a very rough estimate, and on average they stride in at 80ft high. They still maintain something of the age they were born in, redolent of big Bakelite dials and Frankenstein transformers arcing with blue light. They might not be quite Spender's nude girls, but at least Pete Postlethwaite found love amongst the high wires of Yorkshire's pylons in the film *Among Giants* and I do believe there was once a television ad where they uprooted themselves and walked about. And, maybe one day they might gain a cult following; after all, they are objects of mystery – who has ever actually seen a pylon being erected?

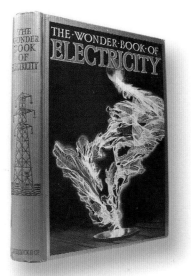

**Alkborough, Lincolnshire** (*above left*)

**Dry Doddington, Lincolnshire** (*right*)

## WAKERLEY, NORTHAMPTONSHIRE

I have looked at these brick and concrete drums for over 30 years and have probably been given as many answers to my queries concerning their use. They are in marked contrast to what is a particularly pastoral stretch of the Welland valley. This is quintessential England: gently folding fields, fox coverts, medieval bridges, stone-built villages. Even the churches seem to rise up organically from amongst the limestone chimney stacks and churchyard yews.

Wakerley looks over to Rutland and its companion village Barrowden across the River Welland, a natural county boundary that here runs through sheep pastures accompanied by the remains of a remote outpost of the London & North Western Railway. Coming along from Harringworth these two orange-brick towers can be seen

across the fields down by the dismantled trackbed and for me this is part of their essential charm. They have a fairly obvious heavy utility look about them, but in the absence of any other ancillary buildings or the usual post-industrial detritus they appear to be as at home in the pastures as the sheep grazing around them.

These drums are calcine kilns for burning the local pale grey stone down into powdery lime. There are two of them (each 70ft in height and 33ft in diameter), plus concrete bases for an additional couple. A tramway embankment and the remains of a tipping dock can be found next to the railway trackbed. To the south the field is humped and hollowed by old quarry workings. Although erected during the First World War they have never been used and the third and fourth kilns were never built. Which is as intriguing as it is disappointing, because as a result we have no record of what a kiln worker's life would have been like here and no memory of how frightening the roaring, fiery furnaces, fuelled by air sucked in through the brick arched openings, would have been to a village child.

## LYVEDEN, NORTHAMPTONSHIRE

The Lyveden valley is a remote stretch of open country
between Oundle and Brigstock. In high summer the
wide empty fields are alive with ascensions of skylarks,
the shallow hilltops dark and brooding with dense
woodland. In bleak midwinter hares course the ploughed
furrows and snowy pheasant shoots are watched over
by little owls in isolated oaks. The curious Lyveden New
Bield looks out over it all, as indeed it has done since the
final years of the 16th century. The most extraordinary
thing is that this limestone pavilion is not a ruin. It simply
wasn't finished, so today we have an almost unique view
of an Elizabethan building in the latter stages of
construction.

The New Bield is one of three buildings built by Sir
Thomas Tresham, a recusant Catholic, to secretly
express his faith. (The others were Rothwell Market
House and the Rushton Triangular Lodge, both also in
Northamptonshire.) It takes the form of a Greek cross
with four equal arms, each comprised of a basement and
floorless ground and first storeys. The original intention
here was for a garden pavilion to sit, as it does, above
the Old Bield manor house down on the lane. It was
intended to be a place for relaxation with boating canals,
viewing mounts and blossoming orchards. These garden
plans have been the subject of enormous hard work and
dedication and are now being imaginatively restored.
So why did the workmen down tools and leave the
New Bield open to the skies? Sir Thomas suffered for
his faith, continually being imprisoned every time an
extremely insecure government sniffed a Popish plot on
the air, real or imaginary. On his death on 11 September
1605 he left debts of £11,495 16s 1d, so his workforce
saw their wage packets rapidly disappearing. And they
didn't hold out much hope from his son either, deeply
embroiled as he was in the conspiracies that led to the
Gunpowder Plot.

An attempt was made by a Major Butler in the Civil War
to remove the stone to Oundle for his construction of
Cobthorne House, a rare Commonwealth town house
on West Street. However, he had to content himself
with only removing the wooden floor joists. The sawn-
off ends can still be seen inside their finely cut sockets.

### MORETON CORBET, SHROPSHIRE

My first view of this spectacular ruin was on a cold November afternoon, a day that had hitherto been beset with thawing snow and uncertain skies. And then, as I rounded a corner of a deep Shropshire lane, low autumn sunlight broke through, dispelling all the clouds and lighting these beautiful outlines like a studio spotlight.

In *Shropshire: A Shell Guide* (1973) Michael Moulder says: 'Rooks wheeling about it on a stormy day give it an air so romantic that one could almost believe it to have been contrived as a stage set for a melodrama.' And I think this is the clue to its enormous appeal. We can read of Moreton Corbet's origins as a 13th-century castle and that the house was completed with a grand Elizabethan wing of 1580, but sometimes a ruined building can be enjoyed as just that. After all, our 18th-century ancestors went to great lengths to construct ready-made ruins on their estates as if part of some painterly conceit. Stage sets indeed. Now these gaunt silhouettes wait to be lit for our own thoughts and dramas.

## TORKSEY, LINCOLNSHIRE

The Roman Foss Dyke connects the River Witham to the Trent, where Torksey became an important medieval town. The river bank was noisy with wharves but the heights of its prosperity were probably over before the arrival of the Normans.

In his wonderfully enjoyable *Sailing through England* (1956), John Seymour moored his Dutch flat-bottomed boat at Torksey in the early 1950s and said of the Trent: '[It] is a glorious river. It seemed to me to be continental in scale: one expects such rivers in India, or perhaps in America, but not in cosy little England. It winds through a great valley of green grassland, a valley in places more ranched than farmed ... One can be lonely on the tidal Trent.'

You still can be and one of the best places to enjoy it is at Torksey. Here on the banks are the impressive ruins of an Elizabethan mansion, a once glorious confection of red brick and stone dressings. It was built by Sir Robert Jermyn and it doesn't take a giant leap of the imagination to see green lawns sloping down to the brimming river and brightly coloured silk flags fluttering from turrets. Now it's just a shell, but no less eyecatching for that. Apparently Royalist soldiers came up here from Newark during the Civil War just to set fire to it.

## CHATSWORTH, DERBYSHIRE

How to make your watermill picturesque: first, choose your location; second, choose your architect. Around Chatsworth the first criteria is easy, with the River Derwent rushing through steep-sided hills. And if you've got James Paine working on an extension for your house and designing your stables and bridge, then the mill becomes a 'while you're here, James' job for him.

The client was the 4th Duke of Devonshire and the original watermill was replaced in 1761–2. The Duke had Lancelot 'Capability' Brown working on the landscape at this time, so this classically façaded building would have been part of a grand plan for the Chatsworth estate. The mill was producing flour up until the early 1950s and exactly 200 years after its completion a severe gale brought trees toppling down on top of it. At this point it was decided to restore it as an eyecatcher, as indeed it is down by the river near Beeley. Approaching from this village the road goes over a hump-backed bridge and then the approach to Chatsworth is to the right. Near this point a footpath will take you down to the Derwent and James Paine's mill comes into view. Very designed, like a doll's house version of a grand house, but a beautiful example of how a working building can be made to fit into the landscape.

## THORNEY TOLL, CAMBRIDGESHIRE

We say the camera never lies, even though we know it does all the time. At first take this looks like a typical farm worker's cottage, isolated out on the fens. It is a rare example of the local vernacular, very basic accommodation under a comforting thatched roof and the kind of place you would expect to discover an eel catcher scraping a living under the vast fenland skies, with the odd glassy-eyed hare hanging up in the lean-to pantry. But pull back a little and the cottage is seen being towered over by an enormous grain dryer and its ancillary buildings, a landmark for miles around. Look out

for it on the A47 when travelling towards Thorney from Guyhirn. This little poached egg of a cottage with its dark hat of thatch is a remarkable survivor. Out on these prairie-like eastern flatlands everything not bolted down or hiding behind a leylandii hedge gets swept away so that tractors and combine harvesters bigger than houses can produce cereals, vegetables and fruit on a quite gargantuan scale. But the silent roads that traverse the seemingly endless sweep of fenland – here and there alarmingly subsiding with peat erosion – amply repay intimate exploration.

## GREAT BOWDEN, LEICESTERSHIRE

It is very rare these days to see a derelict building in the countryside. Invariably they are snapped up and converted into homes for pine kitchen tables and Agas. This red-brick inn has been empty for as long as I can remember, but now there's a McDonald's on a new roundabout next door so I suppose there must be plans to turn it into 'desirable office units' or something. But at least it means it will be preserved.

The Bowden Inn has sat at the bottom of Gallow Hill, to the north of Market Harborough, since the late 18th century. It has a special place in foxhunting folklore because it was here that hounds were kept overnight when the Quorn met in Harborough Country. The huntsman responsible for feeding them always wore a white coat when going about his duties, but one night he forgot to put it on and the pack of exceptionally hungry dogs fell on him and ate him.

Here also was kept a 'cock horse', as in the 'Ride a Cock Horse' nursery rhyme. Gallow Hill was originally a very steep incline (remains of which can still be seen on a tree-lined bank above and to the left of the present Victorian road) and fully-laden coaches and wagons needed a supplementary or 'cock horse' to help out with the climb. At the summit the horse would be detached and returned to the inn. This practice continued when the New Bowden Inn was built further up the hill, a building that can still be seen by the canal bridge.

## WOTHORPE, PETERBOROUGH

The closer one gets to Wothorpe House, the more difficult it is to see. Usually only seen as a group of four towers with octagonal upper storeys hiding amongst the trees above the Great North Road as it circumvents Stamford, Wothorpe needs a certain amount of perseverance to discover. It is all that is left of an early 17th-century house built for Thomas Cecil, Earl of Exeter, whose main home was the prodigious Burghley House a few fields away. So why have another, albeit smaller, house nearby?

In 1662 Thomas Fuller wrote in his *Worthies of England* that Wothorpe was built for the Earl 'to retire to while his great house at Burghley was a sweeping'. In other words somewhere to hide from the dust when they did the spring cleaning. It has also been suggested that this was a slightly less formal place to retreat to; after all being in a house the size of Burghley must have been like living in a small town. I also like to think that they indulged in that hedonistic practice of dividing banquets up over the floors, starting on the ground floor for soup and ending up on the roof for brandy and After Eights.

Wothorpe started to fall down in the 18th century, and I have only known it as a private and particularly dangerous ruin with jackdaws cawing around the silver limestone and dense green ivy. However, now it has new friends and is to be made safe once again.

## HOLKHAM, NORFOLK

Holkham Hall is at the centre of a 25,000 acre agricultural estate. The vast Palladian country house was started in 1734 for Thomas Coke, 1st Earl of Leicester, and after 30 years of construction was completed five years after his death in 1764. Out in the landscaped park, but not too far away from the Hall, is this beautiful brick and thatch building on a slope above a carriageway. This is the Ice House, a superb 17th-century example of a pre-refrigeration store for blocks of ice, once cut at Holkham from the adjacent lake in winter. Along with the church it is one of the oldest buildings on the estate.

Ice, or hard-packed snow, was packed in levels between layers of straw on top of a wooden frame that sat above a drainage channel. A ring in the domed ceiling was probably part of a hoist used to bring blocks up from the lower reaches of the store. Ice started to be imported from America in the 18th century, and early 19th-century records of Holkham show that ice carters dined here in the Servants' Hall.

### CHIPPING CAMPDEN, GLOUCESTERSHIRE

Around the corner from the great Perpendicular wool church of St James in Chipping Campden is a row of almshouses in Church Street (*right*). They were built by Sir Baptist Hicks in 1612 at a cost of £1,000. This little building up on a hill above the town was a conduit house for supplying water to the inmates and its purpose is still commemorated in the name of the road: Conduit Hill. Coming down into the town on the B4081 from the Stow-on-the-Wold to Evesham road you will see it on your right on the field edge. It is not often we see small buildings of this age so completely alone in the countryside, particularly one like this with an ogee-shaped roof and finely ashlared masonry.

## CHASTLETON, OXFORDSHIRE

When I saw Chastleton House for the first time it was late on an October afternoon. I came down a lane wet with autumn rain, past the neighbouring church hiding behind dark yews, until I saw the front of a near perfect Jacobean house behind an arched and pedimented stone gateway. It quite simply took my breath away. Later it was used as one of the locations in two extraordinary films: Tony Richardson's rarely seen *Joseph Andrews* and a television adaptation of Rex Warner's *The Aerodrome*.

Isolated in a field opposite, now mown with National Trust tidiness, is this dovecote. Constructed in the 18th century, it has as perfect proportions as the house, with four stone arches supporting four gables with a central cupola. One summer's afternoon I saw horses sheltering under it from the heat, flicking tormenting flies with their tails.

## LEADENHAM, LINCOLNSHIRE

Whatever our views on foxhunting, we should never underestimate its impact on the landscape. For example, east Leicestershire looks like it does solely because of hunting, with fox coverts and well-kept hedges the result of a unique working partnership between farmer and hunter, so close that in many cases they are one and the same.

Hunt kennels can be found in a variety of locations and styles. Great Bowden near Market Harborough is home to the Fernie pack, tucked away in a back street. The Belvoir hounds enjoy four sleeping lodges, four yards and a special room where the Duke of Rutland can inspect his pack, should he be so inclined. Milton near Peterborough has a castellated Gothic lodge out in the park. The kennels at Leadenham in Lincolnshire (*above*), now isolated in a field to the east of the church, are simple early 19th-century buildings by E J Willson, the same architect who designed the stables at Leadenham House. The front wall has iron railings that delight the eye by curving up to the corner pillars. The central chimney would once have sent a plume of smoke skywards from the hounds' meals being prepared below.

## OUNDLE, NORTHAMPTONSHIRE

Tucked away on an estate in north-east Northamptonshire are these wonderful Georgian kennels and stables. Despite the Victorian additions and a comparatively new roof, they still retain the atmosphere of noisy dogs and snorting horses. Each of the five kennels has a barrel-vaulted brick roof and an arched entrance that opens on to a yard paved in blue engineering brick and enclosed by low brick walls with spiky iron railings and a gate. The stables are now a succession of barns, but two of them still have their wooden stalls and hay racks.

They were built, along with the house at their side, as a hunting lodge in 1820. Lord Chesterfield was a one-time Master of the local Pytchley hunt and he was also a big mate of Lord Cardigan of Crimean fame (see p 47), who lived at neighbouring Deene Park. Chesterfield stuck rigidly to the maxim 'late to bed, late to rise' so that the hunt was often kept waiting for at least an hour. Almost certainly he and Cardigan were frequent visitors here. The lodge would have been an outpost in the hunting field, an overnight stop where the gentlemen could swap the formalities of the big house for the informalities of simpler, less discreet pleasures.

Later the lodge and its kennels became a gamekeeper's home, the barns surrounded by pheasant coops and the walls nailed with menacing steel traps. Above the kennels stretched a hanging loft where the shooting bags were hung, but the barrel vaults still echoed to the sound of dogs with a different purpose.

### HOLKHAM, NORFOLK

Gatehouses and lodges are the heralds for their houses, a taste of things to come. 'Enter here, if you dare,' they say, 'and you will find even more of the same.' Now rarely lived in by aged retainers rattling bunches of keys to open gates for impatient masters, they nevertheless still mark estate boundaries. Holkham Hall has many lodges in the same pale gault brick as the house, but the best is the aptly-named Triumphal Arch out on the southern edge, straddling a driveway outside of the park proper.

Here the gault brick is embellished with round whole Norfolk flints, big eggs of silver decoration called rustication. The design was William Kent's, finally realised by Matthew Brettingham in 1752. What a room that must be above the arch, a perfect place for you to observe the comings and goings down below, perhaps slowly drawing a bow across a cello as you do so.

## CHARBOROUGH PARK, DORSET

The house sits at the heart of an 800 acre walled deer park with a Gothic church and late Georgian tower for company. Thomas Hardy had the tower in mind for the heavenly viewing platform used by the astronomer when he wrote *Two on a Tower* (1882).

The park has four gateways: the Peacock, East Almer, Lion Lodges and, grandest of all, the Stag Gate. This prodigiously high brick arch is surmounted by a stag, poised like a Landseer subject sniffing the air to the west. It was built during the enlargement of the park in 1841 when Mr Sawbridge Erle Drax successfully got the main Wimborne to Dorchester road rerouted.

## COBHAM, KENT

In the 18th century landscaping the parkland surrounding country houses was as much of a craze as it was for their owners to drink vast quantities of claret. Included in the plans were gazebos and pavilions that gave the owner of the hall a vision of Arcadia and if you were really loaded then an impressive mausoleum became de rigueur, a family resting place for coffins that could double-up as a parkland conversation piece. The 3rd Earl of Darnley, John Bligh, desired just such a landmark on his estate at Cobham Hall, but it wasn't until after his death that his dream was finally realised by his successor.

In the late 18th century James Wyatt was a much sought-after architect and he brought this extraordinary building to life on a slight rise in the park in 1781. Classical references abound in the Darnley Mausoleum, with fluted Doric columns, stone sarcophagi on the corners and death symbols like the pyramid roof and reversed torch emblems. Inside are rows of niches for coffins underneath a domed chapel. All of it very, very empty. But this is no horror story of graverobbers or satanic desecrating of the dead. The Bishop of Rochester was asked to consecrate the finished building after lunch at the Hall, but he should have got it over with first, because apparently a serious disagreement occurred

over the emptying wine bottles and the bishop left, presumably telling the earl what he could do with his mausoleum. So it was never put into use and the velvet-covered, brass-studded coffins of the Darnleys never slid into their dark recesses.

I first came across it in an article in the *Independent* in the late 1980s when someone wanted to use it as the central porch of a country house. Closer reading revealed its location to be very near my home at the time and so I dragged everybody off in the pouring rain to find it. Just as we were about to give up it appeared to almost physically come up and tap us on our shoulders. We turned round to see it on a shallow hill above us, grey, forbidding, vandalised with mindless graffiti and surrounded by the rusting shells of burnt out cars.

There are now serious plans to do something about the mausoleum and I hope it's not too long before it is restored and the parkland made more accessible to the public. Maybe something of its dark mystery will be dispelled, but that's vastly preferable to another 50 years of utter neglect, an empty temple of the dead suffering abuse in the Kent countryside.

## FINEDON, NORTHAMPTONSHIRE

This round tower sits on a bend of the A510 between Cranford and Finedon. On its side is an elegantly-lettered panel that celebrates the Duke of Wellington's military victory in 1815. The tower was probably started two years earlier when the local Woodford estate was bought by General Charles Arbuthnot. He was a friend of Wellington, who remarked that the surrounding terrain was very similar to the Waterloo field. Steps inside lead up to a little platform round the central chimney and one can imagine Wellington up here with Arbuthnot, pointing out his Waterloo strategies with his cane.

Later in the century the remote tower became an inn – 'The Round House' – and the field opposite became the location for notorious brawling and dog racing. By 1895 these activities had become formalised into the Waterloo Victory Social Club, which was relocated to Finedon and became known locally as 'The Pam' after Panorama.

PANORAMA

# WATERLOO
# VICTORY
## June 18
## A. D.
## 1815

forgotten parishes, lonely hymns

### BATCOMBE, DORSET

I first saw this isolated church in a black-and-white photograph by John Piper in *Dorset: A Shell Guide* (1966). Michael Pitt-Rivers' text described the church as 'folded under Batcombe Hill and approached by narrow, winding, sunken and often unsignposted lanes'. There was something eerily romantic about it, with its back up against the downs and a seemingly blind window up on the west side of the tower. Of course the name helped and when I saw St Mary Magdalene for the first time I was not disappointed, as one can so often be when one relies on out-of-date guidebooks. It has the look of a church where a bride might be shot at the altar, *Lorna Doone*-style.

There is a curious tale, redolent of Baron Munchausen, of a local squire known as 'Conjuring Minterne', who rode his horse off the down and, in the process, displaced a pinnacle from the church tower. At the time there was a Minterne Chapel adjoining the building and he requested that he be buried neither inside nor outside the church. Consequently he was buried half in and half out of the chapel. The chapel is no more, having been removed as a result of the questionable Victorian craze for 'restoration'. But curiously the tale has a more veracious echo over in Portesham where the tomb of William Weare is placed equally on both sides of the south wall of the church.

### ISLINGTON, NORFOLK

This landmark is on the coastal run to Norfolk, close by a roundabout that marks the end of a long stretch of dual carriageway between Wisbech and King's Lynn. St Mary's church sits out in the fields, variously surrounded by sugar beet, potatoes and the continual turning over of the plough. Apart from the obvious curiosity of a name more familiar to Londoners, Islington – or less confusingly Tilney-cum-Islington – seems to have slowly disappeared only to reappear on the map. An early 17th-century hall shared the grounds with St Mary's in a heron-haunted wood, but it was burnt out in the 1970s. The redundant church would have folded itself into the fields long ago if its ruination hadn't been halted in 1972; now the tower and chancel are roofed, the latter containing monuments to the local Bagge family. The church bears great testament to the admirable work of the Churches Conservation Trust (formerly the Redundant Churches Fund), without whom many churches would either disappear or be turned into something inappropriate like a rave venue. They presently care for over 330 buildings.

## GREAT PACKINGTON, WARWICKSHIRE

Where are we? On a vast Russian plain with the wind carrying the distant strains of a balalaika to us? Or somewhere in Italy, hot and lonely in the early evening sun? No, for we are between Coventry and Birmingham, bordered by the more prosaic pleasures of the M6 and the A45. The church of St James at Great Packington is reckoned to be the most important late 18th-century church in England and one that marks the start of a truly international neoclassical style. The first sight of its four weather vanes flashing in the trees way out in an empty park tempts the romantic to feel the past suddenly becoming much closer, particularly as shadows start lengthening from the isolated oaks. The four corner towers in brick and stone with shallow lead domes, the pediments on all sides. Byzantine, forbidding.

The reason for its construction here is as remarkable. The 4th Earl of Aylesford commissioned James Bonomi to design a church to celebrate the return to sanity of George III in 1789, as good a reason as any. St James Great Packington should be much more well known and celebrated. It's one of those buildings you can't help stopping and looking back at over your shoulder as you walk away.

## KIRKSTEAD ABBEY, LINCOLNSHIRE

This sliver of a building – in a remote Lincolnshire field near Woodhall Spa – is at the other end of the ecclesiastical scale both stylistically and spiritually. How can the mind put this one back to its former glory, or magic the curved ceiling ribs to spring back out to fulfil their original purpose. The dramatic, slender remnant stands like an accusing finger amongst the sheep that utilise it, somewhat dangerously perhaps, as a rubbing post. This impressive fragment of a Cistercian abbey is the south-eastern angle of the south transept, the only significant remains of a monastery built here in 1189. The Cistercians were shrewd businessmen and Kirkstead wool fetched the second highest price in the county.

The antiquarian William Stukeley came here in the early 18th century and found much more than survives today. England is full of the barely discernible remains of monastic buildings, their stone recycled in nearby buildings and walls or swallowed back up into the earth from whence they came, leaving in most cases only a series of shadowy rectangles to be traced in the fields.

## TIXOVER, RUTLAND

The River Welland makes a slow meander on its progression out to the Wash, marking as it does here the boundary between Northamptonshire and Rutland. The village of Tixover once clustered to the north of this 12th-century church, but now it is surrounded by quiet fields and can be reached by a footpath from the present village up on the main road. The Black Death, first suffered in England in 1348–50, wiped out the population here as in so many places.

That great chronicler of the English landscape, W G Hoskins, once wrote that Tixover churchyard is 'a pleasant place for an afternoon doze. It is very peaceful: the only sound the sighing of a gentle wind along the grasses of the Welland valley.' I've wanted to come here and drink a good claret in the shade of the churchyard trees with equally good friends, reading and remembering his writings, but always feared a reprimand by the Diocesan Police. For your own visit, do remember to pick up the key in the village before you indulge in these simple delights in this memorable corner of an unforgettable county.

## WOOD WALTON, CAMBRIDGESHIRE

St Andrew's Church is at least a mile and a half from its village, Wood Walton.
A pleasing mix of the Decorated and Perpendicular, it sits remote and magnificent
out in the Cambridgeshire fields. You wouldn't come down here unless you were
on a church crawl or visiting the nearby Manor Farm, but in fact this church has
been gazed upon, albeit momentarily, by hundreds of thousands of people.

St Andrew's is just a few yards from the main King's Cross to Edinburgh railway
line. It is such a well-known landmark in daylight that homeward-bound
Peterborough commuters will start to close down their laptops or fold up their
*Evening Standards* as soon as it comes into view. Unless, of course, you're friends
of mine who sleep the whole way with their mouths open and wake up in
Doncaster.

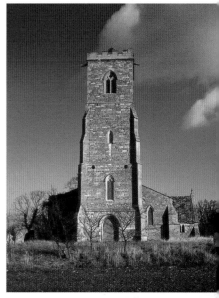

When I first came down here the churchyard was very overgrown, with
gravestones leaning precariously and the church itself encrusted in musty despair.
A recent visit revealed that love and care had returned and the churchyard at
least was trimmed and tidied up. What must it have been like for the parishioners
when the first trains rattled by in 1850 on the newly opened Great Northern
Railway? 'The day thou gavest Lord is ended' counterpointed by shrill whistles,
funerals billowed in white smoke. And then, much later, choir boys rushing out to
watch the *Flying Scotsman* shriek by.

## ST ENODOC, CORNWALL

*The children climb a final stile to church:*
*Electoral Roll still flapping in the porch –*
*Then the cool silence of St. Enodoc'*

John Betjeman *Sunday Afternoon Service in*
*St Enodoc Church, Cornwall*

Sir John Betjeman is buried in the little churchyard of St Enodoc's, his grave marked by a slice of Delabole slate. There are those who think the design engraved on its surface is completely over-the-top, with its fanciful loops and swirls, and completely out of character. I think the critics should see the frontispieces and typography he employed on his early *Shell Guides* and, in any case, I think he would have enjoyed the joke.

But this is not the reason for the appearance of St Enodoc's here. It's rare to see a church spire in Cornwall and up until 1863 this was the only visible part of the church. The rest was covered over in sand, such is the proximity of Daymer Bay. This 13th-century slate spire guided priests to the church, where they would lower themselves down by rope into the interior in order to say prayers. This feat was accomplished every year to comply with conditions to be met in order for the church to be kept open. Restoration brought new life, free from sand. But the sea is always near and in the churchyard wall is a little hut surrounded by tamarisks that I was once told was for storing the corpses of drowned sailors.

## SHOTESHAM, NORFOLK

There were once four churches serving four parishes in the Shotesham area. They were combined in 1731, but two of the churches were already in ruins. St Mary's is in the village proper and St Botolph's is just a summer evening's shadow to the north. South-west of the village is a little sunken lane leading to the Hall and the subjects of this photograph – All Saints at the top and in front the ruinous St Martin's – can be found here.

The tower of St Martin's is the classic ivy-clad ruin that would have made an 18th-century poet take doses of industrial strength laudanum. The remains of the nave are now very low as one more Norfolk church is slowly reclaimed by the landscape that gave it birth in stone and flint. Once, the county boasted over 900 churches, which means that every three square miles would have seen a tower rising above the crops. Most were larger than any local congregation could have filled and many were always strangely and deliberately isolated, and not just because a plague had carried off the parishioners and caused a village to die.

## BROTHERHOUSE BAR, LINCOLNSHIRE

The billiard table landscapes of the Fens are dotted with neat Georgian farms, empty pumping stations with tall chimneys and Victorian chapels that only ever served a handful of worshippers. Until recently this tiny Wesleyan Chapel actually stood on a roadside verge to the south of Spalding. In the photograph you can see it gently leaning towards the fields, neglected, forgotten and little more than a haunt for jackdaws. I wonder when the last hymn was sung here. If you go down the lane now it's as though it had never existed, but when I came across the pile of bricks after the demolition I saved one for posterity.

railway ghosts, tunnelling winds

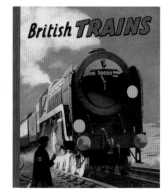

Those with a fondness for railways (and I don't only mean those who loiter around platform ends with plastic lunch boxes and books of locomotive numbers) will take great pleasure in what's left of our once fabulous wealth of railway architecture. Many Victorian stations still appear much as they were built, and preserved lines recreate a rose-tinted halcyon past with freshly painted signal boxes and smart rows of fire buckets. These survivors are only the tip of a vast iceberg that was once Britain's railways. At the height of the system, nobody in England was more than 12 miles from a station, an immensely practical infrastructure unequalled anywhere else in the known universe, much of it now abandoned or destroyed. But out in the fields and down country lanes reminders of railway branch lines that reached out into the heart of every community can still be found.

### JOHN O' GAUNT, LEICESTERSHIRE

Out in the hedgeless fields in Leicestershire is this bridge at Marefield Junction. Here the tracks emanating from Leicester's Belgrave Road station met the Market Harborough to Melton Mowbray line in remote country near the hamlet of John o' Gaunt. A small dairy here once dispatched three or four tankers of milk to London *every* day. All of it now gone, except for the overgrown embankments and lonely survivors like this bridge and a nearby orange-brick viaduct.

### FORDHAM, NORFOLK

The branch line from Downham Market to Stoke Ferry closed to passengers in 1930. The following year a light railway order was made so that freight could still be carried, notably sugar beet. The men from the Ministry then argued that Crossing No. 6 (Causeway) should be dismantled as locomotives could easily be seen approaching through the trees. Thankfully this idea was not implemented and the crossing gate survives here in Fordham due to part of the line once being used by a sugar factory on the banks of the River Wissey.

### OUNDLE, NORTHAMPTONSHIRE

Seconds after leaving Oundle for Peterborough the Nene Valley line crossed a lane winding its way to the riverside villages of Cotterstock and Tansor. In 1962 Dr Beeching wrote the line off in his blinkered report. The level crossing gates disappeared, but the two posts still firmly plant themselves on the grass verges, their purposeful hooks perhaps waiting to once again give their support to a badly needed railway renaissance.

## LEICESTERSHIRE FIELDS

These corrugated-sided wagons are a great favourite with Leicestershire farmers. Minus their wheels and chocked up on brick piers, or just laid straight down on a field headland, they continue to be protective shelters for the paraphernalia of agricultural business. Often they will be used as weatherproof stores for horses' fodder, or even as an outlying stable for a pony. The collection of them at a farm near Great Bowden shows the owner's sense of humour in an alignment emulating their previous life, a train of refrigerated bananas perhaps, hurtling across a sheep pasture, frozen in time.

A vast stockpile of wagons at Medbourne station in the Second World War were suddenly found to be surplus to requirements in peacetime; many of these were consequently dispersed, some finding their ways into the countryside. I am told you can still buy old guards' vans from railway depots; the ones with a verandah at each end would make wonderful summer houses.

## RYE HARBOUR, EAST SUSSEX

Something similar happened to Southern Railway stock, notably passenger carriages. Many disappeared from rusting railway tracks stretched out on the shingle at Dungeness and were made into rudimentary homes – some later extended to become bungalows – on that bleached wilderness. You can still see them, odd conservatories with many doors and windows. This skeletal example still retains its railway character in the muddy nexus of the River Rother, perfectly at home amongst the delightful make-do scruffiness of Rye Harbour.

Redundant coaches were once pressed into service as camping coaches, parked on disused sections of tracks next to rural stations. Introduced in 1933 a family could have a self-catering holiday for £3 a week. I think we should bring them back, but somehow I don't think it would be the same in a carriage where you couldn't open the windows and that had 'GoSprint' or whatever scrawled all down the side.

**GLASTON, RUTLAND** (*left*)

There is a blue brick ventilator beside the A47, high above the Glaston Tunnel on the line between Kettering and Manton Junction. At one time you could sit above the Welland Valley and see steam trains crossing the awe-inspiring viaduct at Harringworth, also in blue brick, and then turn round to see a plume of exhaust smoke float out of this chimney.

**MORLEY, WEST YORKSHIRE** (*bottom left*)

One of the three ventilators serving the tunnel between Morley and Dewsbury provides local colour down on the farm at Howley Hall. Uncompromising Yorkshire style in local stone is offset by a splash of colour from that other 'pastoral peculiar', the abandoned item of farm machinery.

**KILSBY TUNNEL, NORTHAMPTONSHIRE** (*right*)

On either side of the A5 south-east of Rugby are these vast brick drums, castles without doors or windows, implacable and magnificent. They are the main ventilating chimneys for the Kilsby Tunnel deep below the ground, a tricky engineering feat in the building of the London & Birmingham Railway in 1835. Robert Stephenson encountered the same quicksand that had bedevilled construction of the nearby Grand Union Canal in 1809, but he eventually triumphed with the completion of what was then, at 2,400 yards, the longest railway tunnel ever attempted. The tunnel spoil can be seen making tumuli in the fields surrounding them.

The construction of the tunnel and ventilators has achieved mythic status in the annals of navigation. The navvies fought not only the elemental geology of the tunnel but also themselves. Constant fights broke out and three workers were killed, not by falling debris but by the simple expedient of trying to jump, one after the other, over the ventilator shafts before the castellated chimneys were built. Over a million bricks were used in each and they do say that the pub in Kilsby village was built with them too in the style of 'do your driveway, guv' tarmac gangs.

### CARDINGTON, BEDFORDSHIRE

One of my father's favourite landmarks were these two gigantic sheds standing alone in an otherwise featureless Bedfordshire landscape. He would always point them out to me as a child from the train taking us on day trips to London, and with good reason. As a young man he had witnessed the contents of one of these gargantua, the airship R101, as it slowly lumbered up to a tall mooring mast. Its almost indescribable bulk was brought into position with the help of ant-like figures attached to guiding ropes, their feet doubtless slipping and sliding on the grass like a tug-of-war team. His Kodak Brownie box camera captured the moment on sepia squares of paper that graced the family album before mysteriously disappearing.

The Cardington airship hangars are 812ft long and 275ft wide. Nelson's Column, at 170ft, could fit inside easily and upright, should there be a need. The steel doors on each are opened by motors running on their own railway track. One hangar was built here in 1917 at a cost of £110,000; the other, remarkably, was brought here in 1926 from Pulham St Mary in Norfolk. At the same time the original hangar was enlarged to take the ill-fated R101.

This prodigious airship achieved everlasting fame, as much for its immense size and capabilities as for its tragic demise in a muddy French field near Beauvais on its maiden voyage to India on 5 October 1930. The dead from this terrifying disaster are buried in a common grave opposite Cardington church, where the tattered remains of the RAF ensign rescued from the wreckage can be seen on the south wall.

## BALDERTON, NOTTINGHAMSHIRE

If you hang around airfield perimeter fences then you know that this is English Electric Lightning F.2A XN728. It is a surviving example of one of the first, and last, all-British supersonic fighters that saw service with the RAF from 1960–88. They were nicknamed Twin-Tubbers due to the double engine exhausts at the rear.

So how did it come to land in a field at the side of the A1 in Nottinghamshire? The Lightning was brought here in 1983 as an eyecatcher for a scrapyard and since the yard's demise it has been abandoned to rot away. To transport it here the wings and tail were cut off and then reassembled using sheet metal and girders, all of which are rusting severely. The scrapyard has gone, leaving the Lightning alone in a field, spattered with spraycan graffiti. You can find it on a back lane that meanders out of the back of Balderton, though you'll need a good map to find it. But at least it's perfectly visible from the southbound slow lane of the A1, just before the Balderton turn for Newark. It looks extremely vulnerable for an aircraft that probably screamed up and down the old East–West border of Germany and my apologies if it's disappeared. A near-perfect example is preserved at RAF Boscombe Down in Wiltshire.

## CHURCHFIELD, NORTHAMPTONSHIRE

Sometimes one comes across something so extraordinary, so
incongruous, one has to make searching enquiries. A one-eyed pastiche
of Thomas the Tank Engine with a ghastly baring of white teeth sits in the
long grass by the corner of an immense wood. I must confess now that
I know this Thomas very well as he lives quite close by my home and
demanded to be included in my list of 'pastoral peculiars'.

He started life running trackless around the Peterborough showground,
towing a carriage for extra passengers, a cobbled-together assemblage of
brightly painted plywood on rubber tyres. What the Fat Controller would
have said is probably best left to the imagination. On retirement from
show business the possibilities for another life were picked up by my
neighbour. What better vehicle for transporting shooting parties around
the local fields. By this time Thomas was towed behind a frighteningly
large green and yellow tractor, so noisy that cries from shooting-coated
men were lost on chill winds as one of their number inevitably fell out on
to the road. He was also pressed into service as a transport-of-delight
for children's birthday parties, feathered blowers being tooted out of the
windows as it trundled along the valley.

Sadly, Thomas's days are numbered as he awaits shunting into the dark
of the final train shed, but it is fitting that he is remembered here, a
brilliant kingfisher flash of colour in the green countryside that brought
surreal childish pleasure to so many.

## FLAG FEN, CAMBRIDGESHIRE

Farm machinery is often abandoned near where it last ploughed a
furrow, turned a swathe of hay or threw a divot of manure high into the
air. For some time this wonderful faded-red Massey Ferguson combine
harvester sat isolated in a fenland field near Peterborough, as much a
part of the landscape as a scarecrow or folly tower.

## SNETTISHAM, NORFOLK

English roads of the 1920s and 1930s became so littered with advertising messages aimed at passing motorists that legislation had to be brought in to kerb the enthusiams of manufacturers and their agents. Even in remote country areas one could come across something outrageous and out-of-scale shouting over the hedgerows. The summit of Shap Fell on the A6 was marked by a tall scaffolding tower with a clock on it advertising KLG plugs and two cut-out wooden men in white overalls carrying a ladder between them marched around the fields next to railways promoting Hall's Distemper.

We don't see anything too outlandish these days, although I note the depressing trend to put hoardings into fields at the side of motorways, not so much for the things themselves (a side of an old cattle truck advertising a Farmer's Market can be charming), but for the banality of the messages. Who but office supply managers on the M6 Toll can get excited about where to get self-adhesive labels?

Every now and then though, something comes into view that makes everyone but the most churlish raise at least a smile if not an outright guffaw. Probably more at home in America on an interstate highway, where they've made a fine art of these things with filling stations made out of old B52 bombers and takeaways in the shape of pink elephants, this giant plastic strawberry is the perfect medium for advertising a pick-your-own farm. It doubles up as the payment kiosk in season and you'll find it on the A149 between King's Lynn and Hunstanton in Norfolk.

## BRINKLOW, WARWICKSHIRE

What fun! This revolving advertisement for a County Rally, designed and built by the Warwickshire Young Farmers Club, is an utterly brilliant and successful sign. It was temporary but instantly effective as a notice for passers-by on the Fosse Way between Brinklow and Bretford.

## WISBECH, CAMBRIDGESHIRE *(bottom left)*

This big red fish swims in an orchard at the side of the A47, a classic example of a landmark for children to look out for on long journeys. The smaller people in my family watch for this sign for Walsoken Aquatics when we haul over to the Norfolk coast. As much as for the colour and shape, I also like the arrow doubling-up as the fish's mouth and the fresh immediacy of the hand-drawn lettering.

## SUTTON BRIDGE, LINCOLNSHIRE

When one thinks of English ports, top of the mind will probably be harbours the size of Dover, Felixstowe and Liverpool. But all round our coastline are many and varied little ports, all of them potential gateways to the country. One of the least known must be here at Sutton Bridge, a modest but nonetheless very busy quayside to be found on the River Nene a few miles in from the Wash. Quite large ships, often with unpronounceable Dutch names, are able to navigate up to Port Sutton Bridge with cargoes as varied as turpentine and grain, but they can also continue through the amazing swing-bridge that crosses the A17 Boston to King's Lynn Road up to Wisbech, in medieval times a coastal town in its own right.

Running south–south-west from Sutton Bridge is a road that follows the Nene for almost two miles before it turns away for the remarkably named hamlet of Tydd Gote. Out on this road you will notice this corker of a sign, so if it's night and you're confronted by 3,000 tons of tanker bearing down on you, you'll know what to do.

And so our all-too-brief tour of 'pastoral peculiars' comes to an end. It could be so much longer; there is always something buried in a hedgerow to discover, an isolated building to catch the eye, puzzles to demand solutions. I could have filled a book just with the names we attach to country lanes, and doubtless someone else has, but here is just a selection of the enigmas I came across in my travels.

**TYDD GOTE, CAMBRIDGESHIRE**

Only just squeezing into the most northern tip of the county, this is a hamlet on the banks of the Nene, close to where anchors probably did foul in the tidal mud.

**RYE, EAST SUSSEX**

An appropriately dark lane in the Tillingham valley near Rye. We were hungry and looking for a particular pub and my travelling companion hoped that this sign wasn't an omen.

**EXTON, RUTLAND**

'Puddingbag' is one of many names given to that black and white marauder, the magpie. But it could mean something very different here in Exton.

**UPPER BRAILES, WARWICKSHIRE**

What happened at Caution Corner near Upper Brailes? Is it anything to do with the fact that a funeral director's premises can be found on the same corner?

**WOODNEWTON, NORTHAMPTONSHIRE** *(above left)* **AND SUDBOURNE, SUFFOLK** *(above right)*

Temporary signs can often produce their own little wry amusements, abbreviated directions that possibly only the well-informed will understand. A few years ago the AA attached their yellow signs to our local signposts with the mysterious legend 'The Host of Angels' followed by an arrow, and here, near Sudbourne, Emily Brontë's noisy Yorkshire crags are transported to quiet Suffolk.

### SOUTHERY, NORFOLK

This sign speaks for itself really. We wanted to take it home with us and nail it up outside the vet's.

## FURTHER READING

The following titles are books that I found most useful in putting together *Pastoral Peculiars*. Some will be out of print, all are worth seeking out.

Barton, S 1972 *Monumental Follies*. Worthing: Lyle Publications

Biddle, G 2003 *Britain's Historic Railway Buildings*. Oxford: Oxford University Press

Coleman, T 1965 *Railway Navvies*. London: Hutchinson

Cope, J 1998 *The Modern Antiquarian*. London: Thorsons

Hillier, B 2002 *John Betjeman: New Fame, New Love*. London: John Murray

Jones, B 1953 *Follies and Grottoes*. London: Constable

Michell, J 1973 *The Old Stones of Land's End*. Port Eliot: Elephant Press

Mott, G and Aall, S S 1989 *Follies and Pleasure Pavilions*. London: Pavilion

Pevsner, N et al *The Buildings of England* series, Harmandsworth and New Haven: Penguin and Yale University Press

Rolt, L T C 1984 *George and Robert Stephenson*. London: Penguin

Seymour, J 1956 *Sailing through England*. London: Eyre & Spottiswoode

Sharp, P and Hatt, E M 1963 *Follies*. London: Chatto & Windus

Tanner, M 1981 *Crime and Murder in Victorian Leicestershire: 1837–1901*. Leicester: Anderson

Vale, E 1940 *Curiosities of Town and Countryside*. London: Batsford

Various authors, *Curiosities series*. Wimborne: Dovecote Press

Various authors, *The Shell Guides*. London: Faber & Faber

Webster, N W 1974 *The Great North Road*. Bath: Adams & Dart

## ACKNOWLEDGEMENTS

I am deeply indebted to Richard Mabey for taking the time and trouble to write such an understanding and insightful preface for the book. Many thanks also to: David Stanhope, Dr Giles Worsley, Philip Wilkinson, Tim Warner, George Wilkinson, Val Horsler, Serena de la Hey, Yvonne and John Moate, the owners of Old Plough at Prickwillow, Ian Else at Chatsworth, Mark Bradshaw at Lyveden New Bield, The National Trust, Stewart Larque at the National Grid, Emma Grayson at Deene Park, René Rodgers and Rob Richardson at English Heritage, George Hammond, Ian Bishop, Nick Patterson-Gordon, Rupert Farnsworth, Marcus and Jane Berridge, Richard and Jane Gregory, Margaret Shepherd and Biff Raven-Hill.

## RAMPISHAM, DORSET

Easter in west Dorset and an isolated cross on a field edge. I have no explanation for its presence here and, in a way, I'm glad. Whatever the motive, we can all bring our own interpretations to it. The casually placed crown of thorns and crudely lettered identity tag suggest that the Risen Christ has just walked off across the fledgling wheat on a breezily bright spring afternoon, a symbol of resurrection rather than crucifixion.

places illustrated in the text

If you have enjoyed *Pastoral Peculiars*, you may also be interested in other books by Peter Ashley:

**Up in the Wind**
Price **£5.99**
ISBN **1 85074 9108**

**Beside the Sea**
Price **£5.99**
ISBN **1 85074 9094**

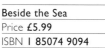

**Letters from England**
Price **£5.99**
ISBN **1 85074 9124**

**Lest we Forget**
Price **£5.99**
ISBN **1 85074 9116**

**Bridging the Gap**
Price **£5.99**
ISBN **1 84159 0479**

**Hard Furnishings**
Price **£5.99**
ISBN **1 84159 0843**

**Guiding Lights**
Price **£5.99**
ISBN **1 84159 0460**

**Grand Unions**
Price **£5.99**
ISBN **1 84159 0835**

**Whistle Stops**
Price **£5.99**
ISBN **1 84159 0452**

**Comings and Goings**
Price **£5.99**
ISBN **1 84159 0819**

**Local Heroes**
Price **£5.99**
ISBN **1 85159 0487**

**Traditional Shops**
Price **£5.99**
ISBN **1 84159 0827**